Freelance
Fashion Designer's
Handbook

Freelance Fashion Designer's Handbook

Paula Keech

WILEY

John Wiley & Sons, Ltd

Registered office
John Wiley & Sons Ltd, The Atrium, Southern Gate, Chichester, West Sussex, PO19 8SQ,
United Kingdom

Editorial office
John Wiley & Sons Ltd, The Atrium, Southern Gate, Chichester, West Sussex, PO19 8SQ,
United Kingdom

For details of our global editorial offices, for customer services and for information about how to apply for
permission to reuse the copyright material in this book please see our website at www.wiley.com.

British Library Cataloguing in Publication Data

A catalogue record for this book is available from the British Library.

ISBN 978-1-444-33506-4 (pbk), ISBN 978-1-119-95061-5 (ebk),
ISBN 978-1-118-35509-1 (ebk), ISBN 978-1-118-35510-7 (ebk)

Set in 10.5/14pt Trade Gothic by MPS Limited, a Macmillan Company, Chennai, India
Printed and bound in Singapore by Markono Print Media Pte Ltd

In memory of my daughter,
Emily

Contents

About the author   xi

Acknowledgements   xiii

About the website   xiv

Glossary   xv

Part 1   **Setting up as a Freelance Designer**

Chapter 1   **The Reality of Life as a Designer**   3
            1   Will freelance work be suitable for you?   4
            2   Experience, qualifications, skills and abilities   9
            3   Working alone, self-discipline and motivation   13

Chapter 2   **Getting Started**   17
            1   Selecting a location   18
            2   Working from home or in a studio   20
            3   Buying equipment, IT and furniture   23
            4   Creating your company profile and CV   25
            5   Planning your portfolio   27
            6   Choosing a working wardrobe   28
            7   Identifying pitfalls and customer issues   30

Chapter 3   **Getting Work and Getting Paid**   33
            1   Where to look for work and how to get it   34
            2   Professional organisations   36
            3   Sales techniques   38
            4   Calculating your rates and expenses   39
            5   Interview tips   43

Chapter 4   **Estimates and Invoices**   47
            1   Calculating an estimate or quote   48
            2   Invoicing clients   51
            3   Travelling abroad with and for a client   53
            4   What your client expects from you   54

Chapter 5	**Financial Matters**	**57**
	1 Choosing an accountant	58
	2 Finance and bank accounts	59
	3 Income tax	60
	4 Bookkeeping and accountancy	61
	5 National Insurance contributions	69
	6 VAT – do I need to register?	69
	7 Pension provision	70
	8 Employing staff	70
	9 Health and safety	71
	10 Insurance	71

Chapter 6	**Legal Aspects**	**73**
	1 The importance of contracts	74
	2 Writing a contract	74
	3 Intellectual property rights, copyright and design rights	76
	4 Keeping yourself safe from prosecution for breach of copyright	77
	5 Confidentiality	78
	6 Keeping up to date with UK and EU law	79
	7 How to find an expert on law in the fashion industry	79

Chapter 7	**Getting Paid**	**81**
	1 Chasing outstanding invoices	82
	2 What to do when a client fails to pay	82
	3 The small claims court	83

Chapter 8	**Planning Your Time**	**87**
	1 The working day	88
	2 Your freelance diary	89
	3 Holidays and your year plan	89
	4 Interruptions and distractions	90
	5 How to stand your ground when unreasonable demands are made	92
	6 Computer timesheets	94
	7 Backing up	100

Chapter 9	**Training and Education**	**101**
	1 Extra training	102
	2 Seminars and training courses for the self-employed	102
	3 Part-time teaching	103

Part 2   Preparing Work for Production

Chapter 10   Design and Development   107

1   Research and trends   108
2   Working to a design brief   109
3   Concept and design, style or shape   110
4   The PANTONE® colour system   111
5   Colour palettes   113
6   Branding   114
7   Tickets and labels   114
8   Preparing roughs   115
9   Presenting your ideas to your client   115

Chapter 11   Presentation and Finished Designs   117

1   Using drawing software for presentation CADs   118
2   Phases of a project   118
3   Phase 1: Preparing presentation roughs   119
4   Preparing a CAD template for a client   122
5   Preparing a colour palette   123
6   Phase 2: Preparing presentation-standard A4 CADs   125
7   Phase 3: Preparing detailed garment specifications   133
8   Compiling the full technical package   141
9   References   142

Chapter 12   Sizing   143

1   Sizing issues   144
2   Access to current information   145
3   Why sizing is different for different companies   146
4   Charts for specific sizing issues   147
5   Creating Excel size charts   148
6   Flat measurements   150
7   Grade increments   151
8   Pre-production sampling and size sets   152
9   Tolerance   153
10   Creating a 'to fit' body measurement size chart   153
11   Creating a garment size chart   155
12   References   164

Organisations and Useful Information   165
Index   169

About the author

Paula Keech has worked in the fashion industry for over 30 years; for 20 of them, she has been a freelance fashion designer, including working as a visiting university lecturer during term time. Her skills include the design and development of garment collections for men, women and children, including plus sizes. She specialises in performance sports and leisurewear and also works extensively on ladieswear, knitwear, eveningwear and maternity. She has exceptional technical skills including pattern cutting and garment construction, plus strong trend, colour and fabric forecasting skills, branding, print, graphics, sourcing and the selection of fabric and trimmings.

> ‘A large part of my success is thanks to Paula and all that I learnt from working with her over the past few years. She taught me how to draw, how to think the collections through properly and just generally to get myself organised. I feel really lucky to have worked with her and hope that her other clients appreciate her in the same way. Her friendship means a lot to me and I really have appreciated all of her good advice.’
>
> Heather Benhrima, Kasbah

You can contact Paula Keech by email at info@paulakeech.com or visit her website: www.paulakeech.com.

Acknowledgements

Many thanks to all those who have supported, encouraged, advised and helped me during the writing of this book: my sister, Claire Risdale, for proofreading the whole book; Shirley Harrison and Laurian Davies, good friends and colleagues of many years, who answered numerous questions and provided advice on a wide variety of topics; my daughter, Hannah; my partner, Andy; and my good friends, Sue Grover and Wendy Boulton. For providing specific areas of expertise, I thank Tim O'Callaghan, David Robertson, Alison (tax advisor), Emma Wilson and David Harrison.

Thank you to PANTONE® for allowing me to include them.

A special thank you to my contributors for allowing me to include their advice and experiences: Heather Benhrima, Paul Bishop, Wendy Burns, Marcus Cridland, Laurian Davies, Nina Faresin, Shirley Harrison, Tim O'Callaghan, Anne Ritchie, David Robertson, Marianne Smink, Suzy Tatnell, Chris Walker, Michele Walker, Emma Wilson and Alison (tax advisor).

I would also like to thank my parents, Eve and Ray Robinson, for encouraging me as a child and teenager to pursue my dreams of becoming a fashion designer and my fashion tutor, mentor and good friend from the Northampton School of Art/Nene College, Yvonne Mitton, for excellent training, support and encouragement.

Many thanks to the team at Wiley and my publishing editors: Madeleine Metcalfe, Amy Glover, Paul Drougas, Andrew Kennerley (Associate Commissioning Editor), Shena Deuchars (Development Editor) and Hannah Clement (Project Editor).

About the website

Not only will you benefit from the expert advice from practicing freelance fashion designers inside this book, but you also have additional online material to support your career in fashion design. These online resources have been created to help you run your business and allow you to focus on the thing you love the most, designing.

Income and expenditure templates have been created to help you balance the books. Use separate documents for your income (Figure 5.1) and your expenditure (Figure 5.3).

Time sheet templates are there to help you calculate time spent for each client. You can use the sheets for each client per week or month, or by design project. The 'clock in and out' system calculates your time in hours and minutes (Figure 8.1), or in hours and quarter hours (Figure 8.3). Both calculate the cost for each entry and the final total.

'To fit' body measurements size chart templates have either a single grade (Figure 12.3) or individual grades (Figure 12.4) for each size to help with your design.

Garment size charts templates can be used for women's, men's, girls', boys' and unisex garments and they include up to eight sizes in separate columns. Increments and tolerances on the charts may be altered to suit individual requirements. One chart has an increment column between individual sizes (Figure 12.7); another single increment column (Figure 12.8); the final has two increment columns (Figure 12.9).

Please visit www.wiley.com/go/keech/freelance to download your templates.

Glossary

A2	standard paper size
A3	standard paper size
A4	standard paper size
A5	standard paper size
Awl	a wooden-handled tool with a metal point for piercing card, plastic, cloth and leather for pattern cutting and grading (also known as a clickers' awl)
CAD	computer-aided design
CB	centre back of a garment
CBN	centre back neck of a garment
CF	centre front of a garment
CMT	'cut, make and trim' – cut fabric, make garment, trim garment
CMYK	cyan, magenta, yellow, and key (black) – the inks used in four-colour printing
CV	a curriculum vitae provides an overview of a person's qualifications and experience
Dongle	a small hardware device that connects to the USB port of a computer for access to wireless broadband or to use protected software
Fabric swatch	a small sample of fabric
Grader increment	an amount of increase (or decrease) in measurements between garment sizes
Grader's square	a clear acrylic tool for pattern cutting and grading, with metric or imperial measurements, grading lines and a 45-degree angle (also known as a grader's set square)
HNP	higher neck point – the highest point on a garment, from which measurements are taken on tops, jackets, dresses, etc.
ISP	Internet service provider
Lightbox	a 'box' with a light under a glass top; when an image is placed on the glass with plain paper on top, the light enables the image to show clearly through the paper allowing the designer to draw over the image easily

Lookbook   a small book containing examples of your work

Mood board   a selection of images on a board that set a 'mood' to visual-
                      ize and communicate ideas in preparation for developing a
                      garment range

Overlocker   a machine that stitches and cuts the edges of fabric for
                      seaming, edging or hemming – the threads cover the edge
                      of fabric

Pattern notcher   a metal tool for pattern cutting and grading that makes
                      'notches' in card or paper

QC   quality control

Stitch un-picker a small tool used for un-picking stitches

Storyboard   a group of designs placed on a board that enables a client to
                      see how each works together and complements other pieces
                      (also known as a design board)

Tailor's chalk   chalk used for making temporary markings on fabric

Toile   prototype garment made in cheap fabric for fit and to try out
                      a design to ensure it 'works'

Tracing wheel   a tool with a metal wheel with sharp points for tracing when
                      cutting patterns and grading.

Trend board   a selection of images, garment photographs or garment
                      designs on a board that show a current trend in preparation
                      for developing a garment range

VL   a visiting lecturer

Webmail   an email service offered through a website, e.g. Hotmail or
                      Yahoo

PART 1

Setting up as a Freelance Designer

CHAPTER 1

The Reality of Life as a Designer

Note: This book is written by a freelance designer living and working in England; laws etc may be different in other areas of the UK and in other countries.

1 Will freelance work be suitable for you?

The advantages of working for yourself as a freelance fashion designer may seem very attractive. This is a competitive market and the final decision needs to be considered very carefully while taking into account any advantages and disadvantages. It could be the perfect career path for some, but would be unsuitable for others.

During our working lives, the only thing that we can be sure of is that our situations will change. Designers may be single, married, divorced or have children that they want to spend more time with. All these personal situations will influence each designer's career and choices. They could be affected by changes in a current job, by redundancy or by being unable to find suitable full-time or part-time work. Any of these circumstances could be the trigger to consider working on a freelance basis. On the other hand, it may well be that it is a choice that is made freely and feels right. Leaving a secure, well-paid job to pursue a freelance path can be daunting. Only you can make the final decision.

I have been working as a freelance designer for over 20 years. I decided to become freelance when I moved to a new location. Speaking from personal experience, there is nothing I would rather do. I love my work and it gives me a great deal of pleasure and satisfaction, I would not swap it for the world. I have been fortunate enough to work with some wonderful people and on some very exciting and interesting projects that I would never have had the opportunity to do if I were in full-time employment. The freelance lifestyle does suit my rather 'erratic' personality. I have experienced difficult times and numerous problems but these can be experienced in any working environment. For me the pluses by far outweigh the minuses.

Nina Faresin left full time employment to become freelance:

> I think one of the most important things to remember is that, when you work for yourself, you need to be prepared to take on a multitude of roles. Being a good designer is not enough to make a good freelancer. Having worked for a large company for many years with resources all around, it was a bit of a shock to the system to suddenly have to become my own IT department, fabric technologist, garment technologist and sales, marketing and accounts departments. Freelancing means drawing on all your previous experience and bringing all of your skills together to provide a good service for your customer. Use your network of contacts to guide you with the parts of the job you feel less confident about and be prepared to pay for services or training to support you as a business.

Wendy Burns of Wendy Burns Designs Ltd prefers freelancing to full-time employment:

> I have worked as freelancer longer than in regular employment. I don't think there is anything better than having flexibility and variation in my work.

Company politics no longer exist and if work patterns vary I can work at the weekend and take time off during the week. This is great for family life!

Marianne Smink is Dutch and has worked as a freelance fashion designer in both Holland and the UK. She moved from Utrecht, Holland seven years ago and now lives and works in London. The case study gives you her opinion on the differences between working in the Netherlands and working in London.

Case study: Working in The Netherlands and London

London, being a metropolis, is a very inspiring place for creatives; hence it attracts many artistic people from all around the world. The competition when looking for work as a freelance fashion designer is huge. Compared to the situation in the Netherlands, there are very many more design jobs advertised and also loads of agencies offering jobs. The first impression is therefore that it shouldn't be too hard to find work; however, this is deceptive as the number of high-profile people looking for work is even higher. In the Netherlands, I was signed up with three agencies (this was almost all of them) who helped me to find assignments. If I got a phone call from one of them, asking if I was interested in a particular project, there was about a 90% chance that it would be offered to me; in the UK, the chances are probably closer to 10%. In London, if I apply for a potential assignment, there is still a fair chance I won't even be invited for an interview. If I get to that stage, the chances are still high that the assignment will be given to another designer, so the quality of competition in the UK is higher and payment is lower. It's difficult to compare pounds to Euros since the value fluctuates, but when I left Holland in 2004, I was on a daily rate of €320; here I had to go down to £200 per day.

Another difference is specialising in a particular area. In the Netherlands, you're expected to be able to do everything including the design of the garment (men's, women's and children's; sports, casual, smart, etc.), print design, labels, etc. In London, it is the opposite; you are expected to have a specialism, for example 'prints' or 'sportswear for women'. If you say you can do it all, you are not convincing. People believe that you can only be really good if you focus on a small area. Another difficulty is that there are not many Dutch brands known here. Even if you can show work you've done for a certain brand, the companies here are hesitant. London-based brands easily feel that they are different from mainland Europe.

The other way around is a very different experience. If you have worked for London-based brands, it gives your portfolio in the Netherlands more value. London is seen as a highly fashionable place and if you have worked there, it must mean you are good.

(Continued)

My personal opinion is somewhere in between. I find London a very inspiring place and there are too many interesting places to go, things to see and do. In the Netherlands, it is a bit more of an effort to find inspiring places or things to do, especially outside the main cities, Amsterdam, Rotterdam or The Hague. I do agree that if you manage to find assignments in the UK, it does say something about the quality of your work, since it's not easy to obtain work. On the other hand there are, just like in the Netherlands, very many companies in the UK who are very commercial, where it actually is more important to be diverse rather than highly creative and specialised. There are also a few highly creative and interesting brands in the Netherlands, just like the UK. Dutch people tend to be very down to earth and being 'all precious' about your creativity doesn't get you very far. At the end of the day your designs have to sell and the taste of an average person is rather mainstream.

Things to consider

There are important questions to ask yourself. It would be useful to make a 'for' list and an 'against' list to confirm to yourself that this really is the correct choice for you. You may need to consider that if freelance work is not right for you now, it could be in the future. If you are the type of person who relies on their monthly pay packet and are in the red at the end of the month this is not a sensible decision for you. You will need to be very careful with your money and often frugal. This is not a suitable job or way of life for a person who is very 'set in their ways', disorganised or needs constant company.

If you are a student fresh from college or university, it would be advisable to try to gain some industrial experience if at all possible before considering becoming freelance.

Heather Benhrima of Kasbah considers that the most important qualities and skills when employing a freelance designer are:

- Trust – You need to be able to trust the designer's instincts and sometimes be persuaded that their idea is better than yours.
- Organisational skills – A designer needs to be organised and able to follow strict timetables.
- Flexibility – A designer needs to fit in with my timetable, if possible.
- Pattern-cutting skills – This is so important to me and, I think, for most designers.
- The ability to put an outfit together from 'scratch' is invaluable.

Heather says:

I expect a certain level of commitment and involvement from my designer and an ability to see the design through to a perfect sample. I have had three different experiences with freelance designers. The first two designers just thought that their job was to do a few line drawings, fill in some measurements and send me the bill. This is not good value for money and for someone like me a waste of time. It took about two seasons for my freelance designer and I to settle well into our working relationship and to understand one another. Our personalities are quite different and I found my new designer's organised and well-structured working methods an excellent foil to my quite chaotic mindset. We worked well together and, although there were a few sticky moments over the years, we settled into a very good professional and also friendly relationship.

Advantages of working freelance

To work as a freelance designer you need to be adaptable, open-minded and have the ability to get on well with others. You also need to be self-motivated, hard working, self-disciplined and above all very organised and happy to work completely alone for most of the time.

Items on your 'for' list could include:

- working freelance gives many designers flexibility and versatility, more choice, fulfilment and job satisfaction;
- being your own boss enables you to make your own decisions and choices, which many designers find liberating;
- working hours can be more accommodating with your personal lifestyle;
- you can decline work you dislike or choose not to work with someone you consider would be difficult to work for or with;
- the variety of work can be quite diverse and there could be the opportunity to try new things;
- working from home can be an incentive: you save time and money on travelling and commuting as you only need to 'commute' a few steps into the next room.

You need to spend time searching for work, attending interviews and finding opportunities for yourself. This can take up quite a lot of unpaid time. You could be fortunate enough to have a work opportunity offered to you by recommendation, possibly by previous clients. It is however wise not to think that work will drop into your lap, for it rarely happens that way.

Disadvantages of working freelance

Working freelance is very different to being in full-time or part-time employment: there is no job security, terms for termination of employment or financial security, no regular monthly income, no sick or holiday pay. The hard fact is that if you do not work, you earn no money. You may need to work very long hours at times and it can be very worrying when work is scarce. You will need to arrange your own pension and organise bill payments. Many other issues will need to be dealt with as they arise. You will sometimes need to do work that you do not enjoy in order to pay the bills and survive. Not all work will be interesting and fulfilling.

Items on your 'against' list could include:

- loneliness and isolation;
- money worries;
- no one to discuss issues with;
- difficulty in finding suitable work;
- difficult or demanding clients;
- taking work on and finding it difficult to motivate yourself to get it finished;
- meeting deadlines (planning your time is very important);
- difficulty working from home;
- problems paying your bills (even more difficult if you rent premises);
- late payments and cash flow problems;
- clients who refuse to pay and the possibility of taking a client to court for non-payment.

Do not be put off by all of these negatives – not all are all likely to happen to you, many of these issues I cover in this book and suggest ways of alleviating them, but they do need to be taken into account.

Making the decision

It is advisable to save some money before you start working alone. If you start self-employment with a loan from the bank to finance yourself, at some time in the future you will have to pay it back. It is a much more comfortable feeling knowing you do not have debts to start with. During your first few years, you may find it difficult obtaining a mortgage until your books can prove your income.

Work can be hard to get, may come and go, and is very competitive; that is the nature of being freelance. You can be working all hours, evenings and weekends for a particular project and then have very little or no work at all. Nothing is guaranteed. Do your research thoroughly. Try to get your first contract before you give up your full-time job. You can sort out most of the other things as you go along.

When making your final decision, try not to be influenced by other people. This could be a major change in your life or a temporary measure, for example, while looking for new full-time employment. The reality of working on a freelance basis can be intimidating to some, yet exciting to others.

Consider the following questions:

- Do you have suitable experience, knowledge, ability and qualifications to work in this way?
- Do you feel ready to work alone either all or most of the time?
- Do you work well on your own?

- Does this kind of work suit your lifestyle and your personality?
- Do you have the support from your family and are your home circumstances suitable to allow you to become freelance?
- Do you have the ability to make important decisions alone?
- Will you be self-disciplined enough to enable you to complete work to deadlines?
- Can you manage your income and finances well, especially to be able to budget during times when work may be scarce?
- Do you have enough contacts and motivation to be able to find enough suitable work to bring in sufficient income and sustain your lifestyle?
- If you choose to work from home, how will it affect you and your family?

Once you have considered carefully all the pros and cons you will have a good idea if working as a freelance fashion designer is the right decision for you.

2 Experience, qualifications, skills and abilities

Freelance work in the fashion and clothing industry normally requires suitably trained professional designers. There are some working fashion designers who have no formal training, but they are in the minority. There is a vast difference between the qualifications, skills and experience of established designers and those of young designers leaving college or university. The diversity of the fashion industry naturally dictates many different requirements from employers, which can be met by the varied skills of designers. Companies may be looking for an experienced freelancer with a wide variety of skills and expertise in many different areas; others may need a designer skilled in a very specific area. Some may prefer a younger, less experienced designer or a college leaver. This is usually reflected in the fees or hourly rate a client is prepared to pay.

Qualifications

Most employers will require some evidence of qualifications and experience and they may ask to see actual certificates and references. All will want to see examples of a designer's work. Any formal qualification will help you to find work. A degree in fashion and design, an HND, a BTEC or a similar qualification can give potential employers a guide to a designer's capabilities and knowledge. Education is always a good investment and never a waste.

These days, younger designers are more likely to have a degree. Not all mature designers will have degrees, but they could have other fashion design qualifications and have equivalent skills, experience and capabilities of a designer with a degree. Others will have taken a different route and possess no formal qualifications at all. They may have learnt their skills while working within the industry, from a relative, or may even be self-taught. There are some very well-known, successful fashion designers who have never studied fashion at college: a passion for the subject is essential.

Experience

Due to the competitive nature of the freelance fashion market, a student straight from college may find it much harder to get work than an established designer with a good track record and industrial experience. Good contacts within the industry can help. It is advisable for a college leaver to work full time for a company for at least a year or two to gain some industrial experience before embarking on a career as a freelance designer. The first year in industry teaches so much. Work experience during college or university is also an asset. College teaches the skills needed but industry gives the experience. Most employers ask for experience but one of the most difficult and frustrating tasks is to try to find a company willing to give a young designer the opportunity to gain that industrial experience. A young designer can flourish given the opportunity; they can, occasionally, be demoralised by a job or a difficult employer. If you experience this, do not lose heart. Better to look for a different job; the next may well be much more enjoyable and rewarding. Once a young designer has successfully achieved some industrial experience, it should be less difficult to find suitable work.

Skills and abilities

Consider the possible tasks you may be asked to undertake as a freelance fashion designer (see Table 1.1). The designer's roles and responsibilities vary and cross over depending on the specific requirements of the project and the skills, resources and facilities the designer offers. A wise option is to concentrate at first on the areas in which you feel confident, competent and capable.

You need to decide which area of freelance fashion design employment you intend to pursue. It is helpful to list your qualifications, skills and abilities, areas of greater interest and expertise (for example, ladieswear, menswear or childrenswear) or specialist areas (such as sports, leisure, evening, formal, wedding or corporate clothing), achievements to date including any competition successes, computer literacy and competence in using computer-aided design (CAD). This can help to identify the type of work you are most likely to achieve.

Some fashion designers may not be qualified or experienced in graphics, print and embroidery design. For these areas, you could consider undertaking training at a later date but it is not essential as work can be sub-contracted to specialists in those areas if the need arises.

On the other hand, competence in using CAD software is imperative. If you do not feel competent using a computer, it is wise to gain some extra skills within this area by undertaking some extra training. Chapter 9 contains advice on training. Extra work can be added to your portfolio (see Section 2.5) as your experience increases, to illustrate your skills and abilities.

Table 1.1   Roles and responsibilities in a fashion design project

	Client or brand	Freelance fashion designer	Graphic or textile designer	Garment technologist	Pattern cutter	Grader	Machinists	Agent, supplier or manufacturer
Client liaison	✓	✓	✓	✓				✓
Product development team liaison	✓	✓	✓	✓	✓	✓	✓	✓
Sales team liaison	✓	✓		✓				
Client buyer liaison	✓	✓	✓	✓				
Supplier liaison	✓	✓	✓	✓				✓
Design brief	✓	✓	✓					
Research and trends	✓	✓	✓	✓				
Design development and planning ranges	✓	✓	✓					
Roughs or black and white CADs		✓	✓					
Illustrations or colour presentation CADs		✓	✓					
Branding	✓							
Branding design		✓	✓					
Print design		✓	✓					
Embroidery design		✓	✓					
Trimming design		✓	✓					
Swing ticket design		✓	✓					
Fabrics selection	✓	✓	✓	✓				✓
Trimmings selection	✓	✓		✓				✓
'To fit' body measurement size chart	✓	✓		✓				
Full garment detailing specifications	✓	✓		✓				
Technical garment size specifications		✓		✓		✓		✓
Technical garment grading specifications		✓		✓		✓		✓
Cutting patterns		✓		✓	✓			✓
Grading patterns				✓		✓		✓
Sample making and toiles		✓		✓	✓	✓	✓	✓

(Continued)

Table 1.1   Roles and responsibilities in a fashion design project (*Continued*)

	Client or brand	Freelance fashion designer	Graphic or textile designer	Garment technologist	Pattern cutter	Grader	Machinists	Agent, supplier or manufacturer
Fitting samples and making alterations	✓	✓		✓	✓	✓	✓	✓
Lab dips	✓	✓	✓	✓				✓
Fabric & flammability testing etc	✓	✓	✓	✓				
Sealing samples	✓	✓		✓				
Overseeing production	✓			✓				✓
Buying fabrics	✓			✓				✓
Buying trimmings	✓			✓				✓
CMT production	✓			✓				✓
Quality control	✓	✓		✓				✓
Delivery	✓			✓				✓

Points to consider:

- What are the exact services that you will be offering?
- Will you specialise in a specific area or cover a broad spectrum?
- Will you work specifically on the design of garments, including colour palettes, or will you also offer full technical specifications with size charts and grades?
- You will need to suggest suitable fabrics and trimmings for your designs. Is the actual sourcing of these likely to be cost-effective and practical or would it be wiser to only make suggestions?
- Do you plan to include a pattern-cutting service with or without grading?
- Is it practical or necessary to offer a first sample service or a 'cut, make and trim' (CMT) service? If so, will this be based in the UK or abroad? You could link up with an agent, sourcing supplier or manufacturing company for some of these extra options.
- Will you offer consultancy or quality control (QC) work?

Heather Benhrima of Kasbah says, 'It is very important that designers should know how to cut patterns. For my company, cutting well-fitting, accurate patterns is an essential part of their work.'

If there is a particular area in which you are desperate to work but of which you have no previous experience, you could set yourself a project that would illustrate to an employer how good you are likely to be in this area, if given the opportunity. You need to come across as enthusiastic, not desperate.

One of my freelance employers said to me that she gave me the chance to work on her ladieswear brand even though my portfolio contained only branded sportswear, as I was very enthusiastic. I had said, 'Try me. I know I can do it well, and, as it's a freelance position, you can choose someone else if you don't like my work'. The first pattern I cut her from one of my designs was for a T-shirt. When she tried on the first sample, she was surprised to find that it fitted perfectly as she was so used to her first samples needing alterations. I worked for her for the next six years. I loved the work and the ranges were very successful.

3 Working alone, self-discipline and motivation

Working alone as a self-employed freelance designer can mean that you may work in isolation for much of the time. This is not necessarily negative but it can be challenging at times and will suit some people better than others. It is realistic to accept that, most of the time, it is just you and your computer. A few people may find it lonely with no one to pass the time of day with or bounce ideas off, but most people get used to it and you can establish a network of like minded professionals, such as other freelancers who you can meet up with, email and talk to. On the plus side, being alone can enhance your work as it gives you the opportunity to make progress without office politics and constant interruptions from other members of staff intruding on your concentration. Self-discipline and motivation can be a problem, especially if you work from home and are the type of person that tends to procrastinate. I find that planning my working day, writing a to do list, and establishing a daily routine helps (see Section 8.1).

You may find it helpful if you are able to work at a client's premises at times or travel with them to trade shows. You may find it necessary to travel to some shows alone but, if you can, travelling with another freelance designer will help with companionship and the cost (if you can share a hotel room and taxis).

Another way to resolve feelings of isolation is to find a teaching post for a few hours each week during term time (see Section 9.3).

Being your own boss can be especially difficult when you encounter problems, including times when work is in short supply or is unavailable. It is often helpful to join a professional organisation that can give you advice and guidance and may also provide you with an opportunity to meet other freelance designers (see Section 3.2).

Emma Wilson of Smartway Consulting Ltd discovered:

> Prioritising the workload was a problem I anticipated, when taking on five new clients all at once. But what surprised me more was the mental challenge of satisfying so many new individual personalities and demands all at once. Each individual client's company has its own 'personality' and learning to understand these can make the difference between a successful and unsuccessful relationship.

Self-employment means that everything is up to you, from obtaining work to completing the work to deadlines. It can be challenging but fulfilling. The feeling when you have completed your first project successfully and have the first cheque in your hand cannot be underestimated! You will need to search for work constantly to keep up the flow, keep yourself fully occupied and stay solvent. Some freelance contracts may run consistently for many years. That can be a comforting feeling, especially if the work occupies you the majority of the time and earns you sufficient income. Good relationships can develop with the people you work for and if the work also happens to be very interesting, you can find it very fulfilling. When, for whatever reason, regular contracts come to an end, it can sometimes prove difficult to replace them with suitable consistent work and you may find you miss the contact with people you have worked with.

> ' It is extremely important not to become solely reliant on one client at the expense of others. As a freelancer or consultant, relationships, even if they last many years, can come to an end very quickly without any of the legal protection employees would have. '
>
> Emma Wilson, Smartway Consulting Ltd

At times, you may be desperately looking for new contracts; at others, you may already have sufficient work and get offered even more, sometimes so much that you have to turn some down. An option at such times is to ask another freelance designer to help you out. They can invoice you for any work they do for you, thus keeping both designers' books in order (see Chapter 5).

An additional worry can be leaving too much until the last minute. Remember; this is a very competitive industry – you must meet deadlines. Deliver late and you have broken your side of the contract (see Section 6.1). Be organised. Consider your reputation: it needs to be good and it is imperative that you are seen to be reliable. Remember that there are plenty more freelance designers ready to step into your shoes. Do not completely rely on next-day delivery services; they are, in most instances, very reliable but it is not wise to risk any delay. Send work a day or two early to make sure it arrives on time. Leave plenty of 'going wrong' time – at times you will need it. A customer will be delighted if you deliver (or they know that you have completed) work slightly in advance of their deadline and will feel that you are considerate towards their needs. You could damage their business if late with your work; remember they have delivery dates to meet as well. The quality of your work needs to be absolutely consistent. It really must be spot on – always. Leave time to check your work to exclude any errors, preferably when not in a rush to complete it. Be honest if something goes wrong; your client needs to know they can trust you. If there is a problem beyond anyone's control, hopefully they will understand but no one can promise that.

Everyone gets a problem with deadlines at some time but do not promise to meet impossible deadlines, even when under pressure to do so from a current or potential client. Be realistic, honest and stick to the facts.

CHAPTER 2

Getting Started

1 Selecting a location

You may be asking questions such as the following:

- Does the location in which a freelance fashion designer actually live affect their work or chances of obtaining work?
- Do designers really need to live near London or other large cities where more design work is available?
- Is it practical for them to live anywhere, in the UK or abroad?

Nowadays, as the majority of garment designs and technical specification details are illustrated using computers then emailed to manufacturers, it is much easier and more practical for designers to work from almost anywhere in the world. A large percentage of garments are sampled and manufactured abroad so there is a strong argument that a designer's actual location is not really that important. For many established freelance designers, there is no advantage to be gained from working close to a large city.

However, obtaining work can be difficult and where you live does need careful consideration. Being within easy access of possible clients could enhance the likelihood of suitable work, particularly in the early stages of contact. This does not mean that you need to live close to your client, but being within practical and economic travelling distance for meetings and consultations certainly helps. Put yourself in the client's position and ask if it would be easier and more cost-effective to find a designer based in a more central location?

I have been offered contracts not only because I was suitable for the work involved but because I live within easy access to major transport links to London. This is part of the reason that I relocated here over 25 years ago. I found a lot more work options were available to me after I had moved.

Marianne Smink is Dutch. She came to the UK from Utrecht in Holland to work as a freelancer:

> Most work in Holland is in the triangle of Utrecht–Amsterdam–The Hague and is commutable. I did, however, choose to move to the UK and live in London specifically to work as a freelance fashion designer seven years ago as I found London very inspiring for my work and am still based in the London area.

If you are planning to work in a remote location, it would be wise to build up a considerable amount of work with core clients before moving. Anne Ritchie of Anne Ritchie Consultancy, which specialises in trend presentations and event management, relocated from the UK and is now based in Spain:

> I had been working as a freelance consultant for about 10 years in the UK when my husband and I decided to move to southern Spain. I had a good

client base before I left the UK and they have continued to give me work. With good Internet access and cheap, frequent flights to all parts of the UK from Malaga, there have been no problems relocating to Spain.

The cost of living and property prices in some areas may balance out the costs involved with travel. However there are some instances when your location can and does make a difference. I am employed to keep up with new trends; therefore it is important to me that I live in a fairly central location that enables me to do this easily. One of my clients wanted a designer who lived near London for this purpose. She was supplying to the UK and European markets; it was vital to be up to date with any new trends. She lived and manufactured her ranges outside the UK, and needed her designer to be able to travel to the offshore factory and UK and European trade shows easily. The designer's time spent travelling and the costs involved were a major concern to her.

The most obvious problem with distance between yourself and your client is convenience and regular face-to-face contact. Most clients do like to see you regularly for meetings as discussing issues and selecting designs and colour palettes in person is easier. Some clients will be happy with mostly Internet and telephone contact or the use of a web cam to aid communication, as this can reduce travelling costs and is sometimes more convenient for both parties.

Freelance designer Shirley Harrison of Shirley Harrison Fashion Design relocated to a small village in the Suffolk countryside 11 years ago:

> We moved from the Home Counties because of my husband's job. I am able to keep in contact with clients by email, phone and Skype. The Internet has also allowed me to liaise with buyers and factories in this country and abroad.

If your client is based in a remote location they will be less likely to find a suitable designer based near to them but, as illustrated above, the ease, convenience and cost of travel can still be an issue. It could prove to be more economical and easier for them to visit you, however some jobs may require you to travel abroad to work so your proximity to a major airport may be a consideration. Heather Benhrima of Kasbah says:

> Flexibility and the ability to travel is part of the criteria I look for in a freelance designer as I live and work outside the UK. For some designers, the idea of travelling abroad to work at the factory several times a year, as well as trips to trade shows, is a turn off. Others have commitments that make it impossible.

Another issue with location can be your proximity to London or another major city for essential research, which is of great importance to all fashion designers. Information and research are also obtained from other sources, but shop research is vital for the majority of designers.

Research is essential to gather ideas and pick up on new trends. I need to respond immediately to any changes in style. I often visit London shops and unique areas, such as Camden, for inspiration. I need to keep up to date with competitors' ranges with regular shop visits too. Watching films and the plays are very important to me for my work. I regularly travel abroad to visit trade shows, shops and other interesting areas for inspiration. I am looking at clothing in a commercial way. I need to see what people are wearing now and how they are wearing and combining their garments and accessories. I seem to absorb information; I am often, but not always, aware of things that influence my work.

It is debatable if moving location specifically to set up as a freelance fashion designer is wise. Many fashion designers will already be based in a suitable location for work, especially if they are currently working either full time or part time for a company. If you are considering moving to a more central location to set up as a freelancer, it is important to take into account the issues mentioned above. It would be wise to delay a move for a while, if possible, until you are more established. It may prove to be unnecessary to move at all. The distances can often be managed; you do not necessarily need to be centrally based. Some designers live in a very remote location, the area in which they live being the basis of their inspiration and even their business. We are all different, with different wants and needs. A good location for one designer may not be a good choice for another. Choose what feels right for you. Be aware of the nature of the freelance business and take into account that work may come and go, sometimes when we least expect it to. You may be located near your client one minute and then the contract may end for whatever reason and your new client could be located a long distance away or even in a different country! Enjoy where you live and just be flexible.

There is new work to be found in many different locations and a new contract brings excitement!

2 Working from home or in a studio

Although it may be more cost-effective to work from home it will not be suitable or practical for everyone. Available space, living arrangements and family will affect your options. The type of work you intend to take on will dictate how much space and equipment you will need. If you are planning on work that involves only a computer you will need less space than if your work includes pattern cutting and sample making. You may find that a percentage of your freelance work is based at a client's premises and some of your time could be spent abroad either travelling to trade shows or working in foreign factories for a client. It is important to be aware that on occasions you may need to be available to travel at short notice.

Working from home

Working from home is usually the least expensive option and is often easier to start with, if at all possible. If you find your business expanding, you can move to larger premises. The type of work you intend to take on will dictate how much space and equipment you will need.

Points to consider when working from home:

- Are you are allowed to work from the property you live in? Check the mortgage, title deeds or tenancy agreement. Contact your local authority to see if planning permission is needed.
- Does your home buildings and contents insurance cover you for working from home? Ensure that all your computer equipment and any other business-related items are included. (See Section 5.10 for guidance.)
- Do you have sufficient working space? A dedicated area is the best alternative if a whole room is not available. It is not practical to keep moving your work around or to continually pack it away then unpack it.
- Do you have sufficient storage space?
- Will you have consistent, uninterrupted access to the telephone and the Internet? You need to be sure you are able to concentrate.
- Are you likely to have interruptions from family and friends that hinder your work?

> *I have not always found it easy to balance work and family life. Closing the door to my studio at the end of the day and keeping it closed, when possible, during evenings and weekends forms a physical barrier and has been the most effective way of separating the two. I then return to work feeling refreshed.*
>
> Shirley Harrison, Shirley Harrison Fashion Design

It is safer and more professional to meet clients in a suitable public location rather than at your home. Arrange to meet nearby, for example, in the coffee area of a large hotel. A lot of meetings these days take place in similar places. If you are planning to have clients visit you at your home, you will need public liability insurance to protect yourself. In the unlikely event that a client was injured on your property, you could be legally liable (see Section 5.10).

Renting a studio

A positive benefit of renting is that it is often easier to focus on work and be self-disciplined if you are away from a busy home life that distracts you.

Do not choose an office or studio you don't like because it is cheap. You will not want to work there if you dislike it. Give your clients a good impression by avoiding a rundown location or dilapidated studio.

Points to consider when renting premises:

- Set yourself an affordable budget (six months' rent in advance is common).
- What are the conditions that apply on repayment of your initial deposit?
- Is there a lease or a license agreement?
- What is the period of notice and conditions required to end the agreement by either party?
- Do you need to arrange your own insurance for contents and public liability or is it included?
- When is the rent review date?
- Make sure you know exactly what the rent includes: lighting, heating, adequate parking for you and clients, switchboard and secretarial services, telephone and broadband connections.
- Are the toilets and kitchen facilities shared?
- Who has responsibility for cleaning, decorating, maintenance and repairs?
- Are there any extras you will need to pay for, such as business rates, council tax?
- Is there 24-hour access and a security system?

It would be wise to employ a solicitor to check the lease or contract to avoid any pitfalls before you sign any agreement. Ensure that you have a written legal agreement that includes details of everything, such as confirmation of rental costs and review dates, payment dates, your rights and responsibilities, access, any restrictions and permission to use the premises for your type of business. It is also important to make sure that you are fully aware of any liabilities that apply to you.

Self-employed Suzie Tatnell and her business partner run Commercial Campaigns, a design, compilation, book layout and publications service business. They work in serviced premises close to her home:

> During 20 years of renting premises at 4 different sites, I have encountered landlords that range from one extreme to the other. My first office was serviced, with a communal kitchen and toilets and a meeting room, which was included in the rent. The rent became very high, so I moved to less salubrious premises for two years. The toilets were unheated, the surroundings depressing and it always smelled of damp! When the landlords decided to re-develop the site, giving only six weeks' notice, my options were limited. To cut a long story short, and one very awkward landlord later, I have ended up where I started, except I now have a garden office in a beautiful Edwardian House, which is lovely. And I pay less rent than I did 10 years ago . . . Never be afraid to barter . . .

Serviced premises are often the best option for a sole trader looking to rent and will provide a route to a short lease and limited liability. A deposit is usually required and rent is payable quarterly or monthly in advance. A building with several small businesses trading from the premises is ideal; they tend to have full amenities included within the rent, such as lighting, heating, shared kitchen and toilet facilities, parking and possibly the cleaning. A meeting room is an asset and will give a good impression to your clients.

Paul Bishop has been self-employed for more than 25 years. His corporate communications consultancy, Presstige, has been run from home and a variety of rented premises over this time. Here he outlines the pros and cons of each:

> Working from home is fine but when you have a wife and two children, it's a waste of time. That's why, for the past 18 years, I have rented space in a variety of offices locally. It's not always a bed of roses but, on the whole, is better than working from home.
>
> In one of my first offices, I was burgled twice. Then I spent two or three years in a rather run-down building near the local station. I next worked from a client's office on the outskirts of town. I use the term 'office' loosely: an estate agent would call it compact; I called it a broom cupboard. I paid minimum rent in return for producing flyers and publicity material at a cut-price rate. It worked well for a while until my bills took increasingly longer to get paid.

The Business Link website supplies useful information for those looking to become self-employed working either from home or renting premises.

3 Buying equipment, IT and furniture

The majority of designers will already have some equipment as fashion and design is usually a way of life not just a job. When first setting up as a freelancer, it would be wise not to get too carried away buying a large amount of equipment. If you are able to manage with what you already own to start with, you will not be left at a later date with unused or unsuitable items. When purchasing new items select carefully, research the best prices, be bold and ask for discounts, you may save quite a bit this way. Consider sales, seconds or second-hand equipment – you may be lucky enough to find a suitable desk and office chair this way.

Basic design equipment, IT and furniture

A computer (PC or MAC will be a personal choice) is essential. You will also need relevant software (Word, Excel, Illustrator or CorelDRAW, and Photoshop or similar software applications), an all-in-one printer with scanner and photocopier, a desk and chair (preferably an adjustable office chair), telephones (landline and mobile), a USB data stick, a dongle, a light box, a shredder, a cutting mat and stationery basics. A fax machine is not essential but may be useful. A PANTONE® Colour System (see Section 10.4) will be essential to most designers.

Telephone number, Internet and postal address

You need a telephone landline and a mobile telephone number, a reputable Internet service provider (ISP) and at least one email account. A Hotmail account, or similar, is not suitable. A full UK postal address is also essential. This will give your client a professional impression. Your own website will also be helpful.

To provide only a mobile telephone number and a free, webmail email address could imply to clients that yours is not a genuine business.

Pattern cutting and grading equipment

If you are offering a pattern cutting or grading service, you will need a cutting table and tall chair or stool, a graders' square, scissors, an awl, pattern notchers, a tracing wheel, a tape measure, a calculator, pattern cutting paper and, possibly, card and A4 envelopes.

Shirley Harrison, Shirley Harrison Fashion Design says:

> I use large brown envelopes 12″ × 16″ (30.5 cm × 40.6 cm) for my patterns so there are fewer folds in them and I paste a printout of the design onto the front of the envelope.

Sample equipment and furniture

If you are offering a sample service, you will need a cutting table, a sewing machine, an overlocker, a table and chair, an iron and ironing board, cutting shears, tailors' chalk, a stitch un-picker, pins, a tape measure and threads. You will also need basic trimmings, such as elastic, tape and zips.

Storage space

Adequate storage space is a necessity. The amount of space needed is likely to increase over time. You will need space for current work, previous work, stationery, fabric swatches and any other kit. You will also need space for your bookkeeping for the current year and for previous years (see Section 5.4). Wardrobes with shelves make a good alternative to bookshelves as they make the room appear much tidier and are easier to keep clean.

Shirley Harrison of Shirley Harrison Fashion Design suggests:

> Clear storage boxes are invaluable! The A3 shallow depth box is ideal for storing A3 presentation work. I have one box per project or per client so I am able to keep all roughs and design sheets and any other information in one place. At the end of the project or season, I put the lid on the box and everything is there in case of enquiries from the client.

Stationery

You may be able to find a suitable supplier who delivers stationery to your door, rather than having to make endless trips to the shops. Always keep essential items in stock; a lot of time can be wasted if for example the computer ink runs out at a crucial moment when you are working to a tight deadline.

I find small stickers with my name and full address including my international telephone number are very useful at trade shows when ordering samples, especially when I am abroad. If I stick them to the supplier's copy of the order sheet, they are far less likely to get lost than normal business cards.

Choose your items wisely and keep your costs to a minimum, thus keeping your overheads down.

4 Creating your company profile and CV

Your company profile and CV are powerful marketing tools and it is well worth spending time creating them carefully. These are likely to be the first impression a client will have of you and will affect your chance of an interview. They should be well written, informative and of good design to represent you and your work. Some freelance designers use only a CV but it is an advantage to develop a company profile as well.

Do some research before creating your profile and CV. The Internet or library may help. Look at other company profiles and individual CVs, if possible. This can illustrate good and bad examples and indicate what to include or omit. Put yourself in the position of your potential employer when considering the type of information needed.

Creating your company profile

Your company profile is an opportunity to inform your client quickly and easily of the services that you provide and is more specific than your CV. You can tailor your profile to target potential clients' specific requirements, highlighting your skills and services within that area.

Your company profile should be no more than one A4 page using an easily readable size and style of font. Include your name, address, landline and mobile telephone numbers, email address and website if you have one. Title the page 'Company Profile' and give a brief description of your technical skills and relevant areas of expertise. A list of the services that you provide will make them easily visible. For example, you might list:

- research – including trend and colour forecasting;
- garment design and development;
- colour palette development;
- computer-aided design (CAD) presentation;

- technical specification packages (including detailed garment specification, illustration and grades);
- print and placement print design and development;
- graphics including logos, branding and ticket design;
- pattern cutting;
- liaising with buyers, sourcing agents and manufacturers.

You could illustrate your successful past performance relating to a potential client's field by including a short, relevant client list along with a brief description of the work with which you were involved.

Writing your CV

Your CV needs to be more general than your company profile. It should include your experience, knowledge, skills and qualifications to date along with details of your previous employment. It should provide a more general illustration of your skills, abilities and past achievements than your company profile.

It should be concise, no longer than two A4 pages, using an easily readable size and style of font (which could match your company profile). Include your name, address, landline and mobile telephone numbers, email address and website if you have one. You can include the words 'Curriculum Vitae' somewhere on the front page if you choose. The first part should be your 'profile' – a description of your skills, experience and areas of expertise to capture the reader's attention. This can be using short paragraphs under sub-headings, or using a list with bullet points. Below describe the type of work completed for your previous clients including the dates involved. Depending on the length of your career, it would be best not to list every single job that you have ever done, just include a good selection of relevant roles. A CV highlighting and summarising the achievements of a long, diverse career is appropriate for the more experienced designer. A college leaver could include future ambitions to give an idea of the career direction they wish to pursue. It is usual to include educational credentials at the bottom of a CV.

Writing a covering letter

Do not underestimate the importance and impact that a good covering letter (or letter of introduction) can have. Compile your own template in preparation for future use for letters and email applications then adapt a copy for each individual job. It does help if you have the name of the person to whom you are writing, especially if it is to be a 'cold' letter of introduction.

For job applications, state clearly the job you are applying for, include any reference numbers and where you saw it advertised. When 'cold' contact is involved, clearly state the type of position and work that you are seeking. Be concise and specific, pointing out any important factors about yourself, your qualifications and experience that you consider the employer will find interesting and relevant. In your letter or email, list everything that you are enclosing to support your application, such as your CV, company profile and any examples of your work. Include your website address if you have one. It always helps if you have knowledge of and can illustrate an interest in the company, so do some research. Your aim is to grab their attention, achieve a response and then, hopefully, an interview. You could offer to meet them for an interview at their convenience.

Checking the documents

When you have finished creating your company profile, CV and covering letter, check and double-check them for mistakes, incorrect spellings and grammar. Then get someone else to proofread them – this is vital.

Remember to regularly update and enhance your company profile, CV and covering letter.

5 Planning your portfolio

> ❛ *For me one of the most important things is a designer's portfolio. I want to be able to see their ideas and what they are capable of.* ❜
>
> Heather Benhrima, Kasbah

Ensure that you always have good quality work in your portfolio so that you are prepared to reply to any positive responses or enquiries for potential work.

Designers, including those who have recently left college, normally already have work in their portfolios. Students are encouraged to add to their portfolios throughout their college and university years. It is very important to be able to show recent and relevant work. If you feel your work may be a little dated or in the wrong area, set yourself a small project of the type of work you wish to pursue. You could target a specific company or brand that you intend to contact once your project is completed. Adding appropriate work to your portfolio will display your abilities to potential employers.

It is very important that work you display to clients is presented in a professional manner. A reasonable quality portfolio of A3, or maybe A2, size in which to display your work would be a good choice. An A4 size, most likely for CADs, can also be helpful and you may also find an extra mini A5 'lookbook' version useful to carry around with you. Select and mount work with great care. Demonstrate your abilities, strengths and versatility by showing a good selection of your work. Include an example of a full technical specification package, if you intend to provide this as a service. Highlight your interest and expertise in your client's specific area.

When showing projects you may have worked on for previous clients, make sure the work is at least 12 to 18 months old yet still relevant. Do not show any work that has not yet been manufactured and delivered to shops. This will show that you respect the privacy and confidentiality between a designer and a client. It will also reassure a client that you will be discreet if they choose to work with you (see Section 6.5).

If you have work in previous clients' catalogues or brochures, you can include them. This will illustrate how your designs work when made into finished garments. To avoid breaching confidentiality between designer and client, make sure the catalogues are available to the general public, not the newest catalogues before they are launched. Actual photographs of models wearing your designs are useful but consider the copyright laws (see Section 6.3) and do not give copies to anyone. You may want to suggest that a potential client views a website showing garments you have worked on. This will illustrate your skills, especially if you are offering pattern cutting or a technical specification package, as they prove your abilities and demonstrate that your patterns fit well.

You could include research work for the coming season in the form of 'mood' and trend research boards within your portfolio. You may choose to use research from a previous season as an example at the interview stage; this will avoid giving away information 'for free'.

Shirley Harrison of Shirley Harrison Fashion Design says:

> I always try to include colours, fabrics, trends and information for the next season so that companies can see that I am pro-active and thinking ahead. Knowledge of competitors' ranges is also important.

You may need to adapt your portfolio at times to illustrate your abilities in a particular type of work for which you are to be interviewed. You may even be asked to attend a second interview and work on some designs to test your suitability. Be careful if you are asked to do this – it may be perfectly legitimate but sometimes it may not be. Never let any of your work out of your sight at an interview (see Section 2.7).

As your work develops and changes throughout your career so should your portfolio. It is vital to keep it up to date, as you never know when you will get a call for possible work and need to attend an interview at very short notice.

Remember, your portfolio reflects you, your work and your attitude to your work. A tatty, messy portfolio will show that you do not really care. A neat, well-organised portfolio reflects positively on you as a designer and illustrates your professionalism and high standards.

6 Choosing a working wardrobe

Attempting to give designers information and advice on how to dress can be difficult as each is so individual and diverse with their ideas.

Although fashion designers may have a reputation for dressing in an outrageous way, I find many dress in a fairly conventional way with quirky twists or accessories. While design is an art form, industry and business are not and, at times, codes of dress may clash. In certain business situations, a degree of conformity may be needed. Shirley Harrison says 'I believe first impressions are very important. How we present ourselves is a form of non-verbal communication'.

Dressing for interviews

Working on a freelance basis means more interviews than the average person. It can be difficult to know how to dress for them. Although your appearance is the first impression that an interviewer receives of you, the importance of this is sometimes overlooked. Designers are able to get away with many modes of dress that other professionals may not. Some people expect designers to look up-to-the-minute, unusual, quirky, strange, weird or just a little odd in appearance. Are they disappointed if we look reasonably conventional? Do they think we will design strange garments for their range if we dress in an unconventional manner? Exactly what are our clients' expectations of our appearance? Marcus Cridland, sales and marketing director of Shires Equestrian Products, gives an employer's point of view:

> When interviewing for a clothing designer, 'weird' or 'different' clothing is acceptable but I would expect that person to be smart and stylish in their appearance. People's dress code is a reflection of their personality and we are all looking for a clothing designer who can offer us something different or unique that our competition doesn't have. A designer needs to have a smart and stylish appearance, have good personal hygiene, look and be professional and present themselves well.

Heather Benhrima of Kasbah considers the significance of a designer's appearance at an interview: 'The way the designer presents themselves is very important. I would like to see that there is an element of creativity in the way they put their everyday wardrobe together.'

Personal hygiene is high on the list, including clean hair and careful make-up. An unkempt, messy appearance with dirty hair and tatty footwear shows a lack of care and does not give a professional impression to a potential employer, however fashionable 'the look' happens to be at the time. Select your 'image' with great care.

We need to be stylish, smart and presentable with perhaps an unusual or quirky twist. A degree of tailoring worn in an interview situation gives a professional appearance and adds an air of authority. Smart footwear needs to be worn and it is not advisable to wear jeans for the first interview. Consider colour: black is safe and still seems to predominate but wearing colour can enhance your appearance and mood. Wearing only dark colours can feel and look drab; a touch of colour, such as a red shirt, can lift an outfit and improve your mood, giving you confidence.

Dress to feel comfortable if, for example, you will be sitting in a car for several hours, but you do not want to arrive looking crumpled.

Dressing for work

Once you begin working as a freelancer, you may find that you do not need a large selection of work clothing. You need suitable clothing for meeting clients and visiting shows and seminars but, when working from home, you can wear literally anything! Even if you rent premises, unless you meet clients frequently, your code of dress is entirely up to you.

I believe that the way you dress has an effect on the way you feel. I would not advise working from home wearing a dressing gown until lunchtime; it will make you feel sloppy, unprofessional and lethargic. Better to shower and dress. It does not look good to open the door still wearing your nightclothes if someone calls – it gives the impression you do not take your work seriously and is unlikely to aid your motivation and self-discipline.

7 Identifying pitfalls and customer issues

This section is intended to help you avoid situations and issues that could prove difficult, as my personal experiences show.

• Never use magazine images on mood or trend boards that you present, show, leave with or send to a client. Designers should be aware that if they use photographic images from magazines and use them on mood boards that they could be found liable for breaching the copyright of the photographer. If you do not get permission from the photographer it is possible the photographer will sue you. If the designer has done the work on behalf of a client and the client uses the mood boards for their own advertising – the photographer could sue the client, and then the client counter sue the designer. Being sued could cost thousands of pounds or Euros. See Section 6.4 for information on keeping yourself safe from prosecution for breach of copyright.

• Always work to an agreed written and signed contract (see Section 6.1).

• Find out if the client is reputable. Talk to other designers and people in the industry who may have worked with a potential client. They may be able to offer advice on whether they had a bad experience or if they worked well. You could do a company search to find if the directors of a company have any judgements against them – can they pay your invoices? You do have to pay for this but on some occasions it can be worth it.

• Never allow an interviewer to leave the room with any of your work and designs, for example to 'show a colleague'. Always keep your work in view. If anyone wishes to view your work, they may meet you in person. If you do not take this precaution, you could find they have made a photocopy or photograph of your design.

• Each of my designs now includes my copyright details, as I have learnt the hard way. During a second interview, an interviewer once said they would just 'hang onto' work that I had completed with their range in mind. They began to pull my work across the desk and I informed them that I never leave any of my work unless it is paid for. Needless to say, I no longer wanted that job nor did I hear from them again. If a client is really interested in employing you, they will, in most instances, get a good idea of your work and abilities from meeting you in person and looking at your portfolio. They have no reason to request to 'keep' any of your work.

• Never leave any of your work and designs with a client with whom you have not yet agreed a price, by whom you are not employed and with whom you have not agreed and signed a contract. I have been working as a designer for over 30 years. During that time, I must have come across every trick in the book and been caught out several times.

• Be wary of requests to send examples of your work by email for interview and avoid sending them if possible. It is much safer to meet the potential client face to face for an interview so you may show them your work. Reputable companies and recruitment agencies do sometimes request examples of a designer's work along with their CV at the selection stage. Be very cautious of sending your work to unknown sources. If work must be sent it is advisable to use out-of-date work that includes your copyright notice as well as including a copyright watermark across it. Ensure you know to whom and where it is going. Ask for it to be deleted or destroyed after it has been considered for the work.

• Be aware of the importance of a client's telephone number, email address and full postal address. Avoid working with a client who only supplies a mobile telephone number and a free, webmail type of email address (such as Hotmail). Be even more wary if they also refuse to give you a full UK postal address, give just a box number or only direct you to their website. Always check out their website contact details thoroughly. Any reputable company or client will be happy to supply a telephone landline, a reputable Internet service provider (ISP) email address and a full UK postal address. If a client works from home they may be reluctant to give you their address for security reasons. However remain cautious, especially if they want you to work for them without meeting them first or if you have only met them in a public place. Are they avoiding agreeing and signing a contract with you? Where do you send your invoice? Will you be left to pay any expenses involved in the work you do for them? Do not accept a request to send your invoice via email until you have all the above vital information.

• Be careful when sending emails to clients. I managed to send one to a male client with 'Love Paula XX', after sending several emails to my sister. I felt an utter idiot and had to send an apology. Fortunately, he was a client I had worked for a few years and was rather amused by my mistake. It does make me wonder how many times in the past I have done that without realising!

- If you are asked to travel abroad with a client and you do not feel comfortable with them or are unhappy with the arrangements and feel unsafe, do not go. If both parties have already signed a contract and you find yourself in extreme or difficult circumstances you may need to consider cancelling the project altogether. Check your contract and contact your solicitor for advice.

- If a client really does not like the work you do for them you will need to come to a compromise to resolve the issue. It may even be necessary to cancel the contract.

CHAPTER 3

Getting Work and Getting Paid

1 Where to look for work and how to get it

> ' *Designers should network as much as possible to meet people who may, at some stage, be able to employ or recommend them. I believe that if you miss an opportunity to meet with somebody then you may be missing a valuable business opportunity.* '
>
> Chris Walker, Managing Director, Inspired Business Solutions

It is vital to be pro-active and search for work and there is a variety of ways to try and find it. Looking through the appointments section of trade publications is an obvious one; advertising in the freelance services section is another. You could contact a professional organisation (see Section 3.2) to see if they have suitable contacts or join some form of freelance directory or database. This does not guarantee work but it can be very helpful. Specialist recruiting agencies for the fashion industry can be another avenue to pursue; opportunities may be available for contract, freelance, temporary, part time or permanent design work.

I belong to the Register of Apparel and Textile Designers, which is part of the UK Fashion and Textile Association (UKFT), the trade association for the fashion and textile industry in the UK. It is a help and advice service for designers of fashion, knitwear and textiles and other specialists, such as pattern cutters and graders. Companies or other designers searching for designers or specialists are given details of registered members offering the services they seek. Most of my work has come from the register. Many of the companies looking for design input are members of UKFT, which can be reassuring.

> ' *I started looking for a designer when my business began to expand and I knew that I couldn't cope with the pressure of designing alone. I had no training but an eye for fashion and a good factory that manufactured my designs. I contacted the UKFT as I had no idea how to find a designer. I wanted a freelancer, as my company couldn't really justify a full-time designer. They sent me the names of several candidates and I set up interviews at our stand at Pure. I interviewed about five designers and I was the most interested in those that had already worked with companies similar to my own.* '
>
> Heather Benhrima, Kasbah

Research is needed to identify potential customers. Contact companies you have worked for in the past to let them know that you are now working on a freelance basis and also contact their competitors. When you write to companies or brands you would like to work for, target the managing director or the design director. Find out the name of the person you need to deal with and contact them – you are less likely to be considered if you simply write to the human resources department. Your letters should be targeted – highlight something interesting about the company (unique to them) and how you could fit in.

When you telephone, write to or visit potential clients without previous contact (known as 'cold calling'), research the company in advance and know a bit about them. If you visit, remember to take a small 'lookbook' to show off your designs.

Visiting trade shows can be fruitful and also keeps you up to date with current trends. Collect catalogues and buy a show guide, which usually lists all of the exhibitors, for future reference. Ask about the possibility of work, take details and ask for a contact name. The people on the stand will be sales people and won't necessarily have much to do with design. Hotels and restaurants located close to a show venue are often full of visitors and exhibitors. Although a delay on one return trip was an inconvenience, I found myself talking to other delayed passengers who had visited or exhibited at the same show and we swapped business cards.

Search for suitable websites on the Internet. Attend industry networking events and seminars: you never know who you could meet. Try contacting brands, high street names and design companies who supply them. Luck can sometimes play a part: make contact at just the right moment and you could land yourself some work! You may have established clients for whom you work regularly, but it is wise to keep looking for future possibilities. Do not be complacent.

It can be difficult and demoralising at times when you have spent a substantial amount of time and effort trying to find work. You may have written many letters or emails and telephoned many different companies with little or no response. If you get a reply, even if there is no work available at present, you stand a chance of being contacted at a later date. You need to be persistent, thick skinned and never give up. I have had several letters saying, 'We will keep your details for future reference'. On two occasions, a year or so later, I was telephoned out of the blue with an offer of some work.

Read the trade press (including online news and your local papers) and watch TV and radio. If a story appears about a company you think sounds interesting, get their contact details and approach them.

Ask colleagues, college or university lecturers and friends (and possibly relatives) for recommendations. Use business and social networking sites (such as, LinkedIn, Bebo, myspace and Twitter) if they appeal to you; they can be powerful tools for getting in touch with people in 'the business'.

You can also advertise your services in the following places:

- your own website – make sure it is up to date and looking great;
- www.drapersjobs.com;

- other websites;
- your local paper, especially for pattern cutting and other specialist services;
- local paid advertising directories, such as Yellow Pages and Thompson Local; Yellow Pages offers a free line.

Laurian Davies of the Register of Apparel and Textile Designers suggests:

> Contact local papers, TV and radio – put an interesting press release together about yourself and what you do. Send it, with a recent photo, to as many of these as you can – you may well be surprised and get a response! They are always looking for stories.

You cannot always tell if your current contracts are likely to continue. A very reliable company with which you have built up a good relationship may encounter problems. Freelancers tend to have their hours reduced or axed before permanent staff. It is wise to be aware of this, to keep your options open and to continue looking.

2 Professional organisations

To give extra credibility and much needed support, it is worth considering joining one or more professional organisations. The facilities available may include a database and recommendations for work, as well as seminars, training and meeting facilities. Professional organisations may also give access to current information on the Internet and a trend library. Some may offer industry books for you to purchase, possibly at a discount. Attending seminars run by these organisations not only aids your work, it also helps you to meet other freelance designers.

Contact details for the organisations mentioned in this section are in the Organisations and Useful Information section at the end of the book.

UKFT UK Fashion & Textile Association

UKFT is the umbrella body for trade associations in the UK fashion and textile industry. It was established to help these organisations work more closely together and to establish a collective voice to represent the sector. UKFT organises regular seminars on varying subjects within the fashion industry; members of the register can take advantage of reduced rates for them. There are also networking events on a regular basis at its London address. Members have access to business information on a variety of subjects related to the fashion industry, such as training, exports, new European legislation and the environment.

The UKFT Colour and Trend library is located in the Thomas Ramsden mill complex, Guiseley, West Yorkshire. UKFT has invested significant funds to update the library and give member companies access to inspirational trend sources. This seasonal information provides designers with an international perspective on colour and fabric direction at a vital stage of their product development for the new season. Key trend sources are stocked in the library and are supplemented by trend books from leading trade exhibitions such as Premiere Vision, MoOD and Heimtextil, plus several other international organisations such as Masters of Linen and AWI/Peclers. Use of the library is available on an appointment basis to members of UKFT and the Register of Apparel and Textile Designers.

The Register of Apparel and Textile Designers

The register is part of the UKFT. Based in London, it is a membership organisation, offering help and advice on going freelance or improving your freelance business. It also offers the possibility of freelance work.

I have been a member of the register for many years and it has been a lifeline. If I ever encounter problems there is always a wealth of constructive advice and guidance available at the end of the phone. I found it especially supportive when I was forced to take a client to court for non-payment of a large invoice. On many occasions, the register has recommended me to companies, which has resulted in some valuable and interesting work. It has given me guidance on fees and there are conference or meeting rooms available at its premises in London.

EMTEX Designer Forum

Emtex Designer Forum in central Nottingham supports fashion, textile and design students, lecturers, freelancers, companies, retailers and suppliers throughout the UK. The Designer Forum has a trend library, which members can book to use per hour or day. It houses trend publications from Nelly Rodi, Mudpie and Stylesight online trends. Users are allowed to make hand drawings and notes, along with taking printouts from Stylesight, however photographs, downloads and emailing from the resource library is forbidden. There is a members' database of freelancers and companies. For a small membership fee, freelancers can have year-around access to the trend library, their details in the freelance directory and one printed list of all other members. Freelancers can also receive an electronic newsletter that details recruitment, legislation, events, trends and regular job vacancy alerts. Computer-aided design (CAD) training is also available for a discounted fee, along with referrals for website development, bookkeeping and IT solutions. There are various subscription levels, with a special rate for students. Company subscriptions are also available.

I joined Emtex Designer Forum on the recommendation of a colleague. I love the trend library, as it allows me access to information that I would otherwise not be able to afford as a freelancer.

The Scottish Textile Industry Association

The Scottish Textile Industry Association represents Scottish textile manufacturers and designers. It promotes information, benefits and the range of products and businesses within the Scottish textile and fashion sectors through its brand, activities and website, which has an area dedicated to designers that includes news and networking.

Textile Market Intelligence Trend presentations are held twice a year. They are currently delivered by Anne Ritchie Consultancy on behalf of Scottish Enterprise.

ASBCI Association of Suppliers to the British Clothing Industry

ASBCI brings together the clothing industry from fibre manufacturers to garment manufacturers, retailers and people who provide aftercare. They hold regular technical seminars that tackle a variety of important industry topics.

3 Sales techniques

How do you sell yourself and the services you offer? It is essential to make a good impression from your first contact, be it by telephone, letter, email or in person.

Your company profile, CV, covering letter or letter of introduction, and telephone manner are tools to help you sell yourself to a potential client. The way you compile your letters and emails are also important. Be professional, polite and be yourself. Remember the client's name during telephone calls but never be over familiar. Under no circumstance say anything negative about previous clients. Recommendations and references are a positive way to reassure a potential client. They prove that you are competent in your work and able to do what you say you can. Make sure that referees you name (such as, previous employers or college tutors) are happy to provide a reference for you. Keep up-to-date references to show to clients. Demonstrate that you will be an asset to their company.

Look at yourself and your business from your clients' position:

- How do you come across?
- What would you think of you if you were the client?
- Can you do anything better?

Be professional, present yourself well and know your stuff. A client also needs to feel that they can work with you.

Marcus Cridland, Sales and Marketing Director,
Shires Equestrian Products

Try not to come across as forceful or pushy, you should allow a client to feel they are in control and making the decisions. It is best to be positive and approachable and have a friendly manner.

Always follow up contacts, job applications, letters, emails and telephone calls that you have made and sent. Did they receive your letter, application, company profile and CV? Offer to meet for an interview. Make an effort to visit the company's stand at a trade show and introduce yourself: this can help them to remember you. It is always worth meeting potential clients even if at the time it does not result in work. One company contacted me two years after I was interviewed. They remembered me and liked my work: it was not exactly what they had needed at the time but was just what they needed at a later date. I have worked for them on several occasions since.

4 Calculating your rates and expenses

In all situations regarding your rate of pay and expenses, you need to be seen as fair and yet avoid being taken advantage of. There can be enormous differences in what clients are prepared to pay, most will want to negotiate, so leave room in your fees. Consider carefully the fees on offer before accepting a low rate, there is always someone who charges less than you. There are so many variables such as the competition, country you work in etc. You should charge a minimum of half a day, even if you only have an hours meeting – it's half a day out of your working hours. You may perhaps charge different fees for different clients' so ensure you keep accurate records.

Decide what is to be included in your fees. As the additional expenses of any project can vary considerably, it is advisable to keep to your rate and itemise any additional expenses on your invoices. This should avoid any disagreements. Another option is to charge a slightly higher hourly or daily rate that includes basic expenses such as stationery and reasonable telephone call costs.

I had a very expensive problem when a client wanted excessive quantities of full colour copies printed. It cost a fortune in ink and the client just assumed that it was included in my fee. When I asked the client to pay for them as an extra, the client was not happy. I have had similar problems with excessive telephone calls too, particularly to mobiles and abroad. These costs can eat into your fee.

Covering expenses

Take care when any project involves a large amount of expenses. Request an advance payment from your client to cover the estimated costs or you could end up financing their business! In the event that the client fails to pay you on time (or at all), you risk losing not only your fee but also your own hard-earned cash (see Sections 6.1 and 6.2).

You need to keep notes in your working diary (see Section 8.2) of any items and expenses that you incur during a project and save all receipts (see Section 5.4). This will enable you to cost and identify accurately all extras for each particular client and may also help with any disputed costs.

Deciding your hourly and daily rate

> " I prefer to work on an hourly rate but, from a client's point of view, they need to know how much they are going to have to pay me for the whole project. I have been paid in different ways when working for different companies: an hourly or daily rate, a project basis and also on an annual contract. When working on a project basis, I estimate the amount of time it will take to complete and include an hourly rate for any additional or alteration work. This means that I am not being asked to do a lot of unforeseeable alteration work and end up devaluing my hourly rate. I keep time sheets of the hours that I spend on each project, so I can be realistic about the amount of time work is likely to take when I am writing future proposals and quotations. "
>
> Shirley Harrison, Shirley Harrison Fashion Design

It can be difficult to know how much to charge per hour or per day, how much you are 'worth' and what is the 'going rate'. Contacting recruitment agencies and looking at job adverts or the Internet may give you an idea of current freelance rates. If you are a member of a professional organisation, enquire if they are able to give you any guidance. Freelance rates do vary depending on experience, skills, ability and qualifications. I have been guided on how much to charge per hour and per day by the freelance register.

Fees from an employer's point of view

> " Know your stuff and expect to be asked about hourly or daily rates. It is important to know your upper and lower limits. You may wish to offer a quotation to complete a project for a company. It is your choice whether you work by the hour or to 'do a job', but sometimes companies have to work to strict budgets and will want or need to work to a fixed figure. "
>
> Marcus Cridland, Sales and Marketing Director,
> Shires Equestrian Products

Most clients do work to a budget, which you may or may not be happy with (see Section 4.1). As a freelancer, you are only paid for the hours worked so keep details of the actual hours you work for each client in your diary (see Section 8.2). Computer time sheets to record and calculate hours worked are also useful (see Section 8.6). Although you may get a higher rate of pay than a designer in full-time employment, you do not get paid when things go wrong or unexpected problems arise, for example, when your printer doesn't work; some of these unforeseen problems can take up a surprising amount of time. It can sometimes be difficult to get paid what you are 'worth'; I have on occasions accepted a lower fee to get the work. Sometimes it can be sensible to stand your ground where fees are concerned; at other times it is sensible to compromise. It really depends on the situation, the client's budget and the work involved. In the past, I have missed out on work as other people sometimes agree to do the work for less money.

Compiling a year plan

Compile a year plan incorporating all the essential tasks (bookkeeping, marketing, etc.) that you need to complete as a self-employed person. Work out the salary you need to earn each year to cover your personal expenses. Then calculate all the business expenses you are likely to incur during the year. Work out chargeable hours deducting those spent on administration (include writing letters and emails, making telephone calls, attending interviews, travelling, negotiating and attending seminars and trade shows), bookkeeping and marketing. Add a week or so for possible illness, a few weeks for holidays and for Christmas, Easter and bank holidays. What you need to earn, what you think you will earn and what you are likely to earn may not tally, so be realistic in your expectations.

The following example is based on a five-day working week:

- Start with a normal year of 365 days: 52 weeks and 1 day.
- Subtract four weeks' holiday, another week for Christmas and New Year and another week for various other holidays (two days at Easter and one day each for the May Day, Spring and August bank holidays): 46 weeks and 1 day.
- Subtract one week for illness: 45 weeks and 1 day.
- Subtract one day per week for administration, bookkeeping and marketing: 36 weeks and 1 day.
- Subtract five weeks for negotiating with clients, research, attending trade shows, seminars and periods with no work: 31 weeks and 1 day.

You are left with 31 weeks and 1 day, which equals 156 days for paid work on clients' projects. Do not forget to deduct any hours spent on other paid work, such as part-time teaching, from this total. Those can be calculated separately as they may be a different hourly rate of pay.

Table 3.1   Business expenses calculator

Expense	Estimated cost per annum
Rent, rates, council tax, utilities (gas, electricity, etc.)	
Loan interest, hire purchase, etc.	
Accountancy fees	
Insurances: buildings, contents, public liability, etc.	
Telephone and Internet: land, mobile, broadband	
Advertising, promotion, etc.	
Postage and courier costs	
Computer, software, printer, repairs, etc. (include depreciation)	
Stationery: computer paper, inks, envelopes, etc.	
Materials including samples, etc.	
Subscriptions, publications, magazines, etc.	
Seminar fees	
Travel: home and abroad	
Car expenses	
Legal fees: any contract advice/non-payments if company were to go in to liquidation owing you money etc	
Additional expenses	
Total estimated cost	

You can calculate your billable hours assuming you work a 40-hour week (8 hours per day). You may, for example, work from 9 A.M. to 6 P.M., with an hour of breaks, each day. This equals a total of 1248 billable hours. The hours you actually choose to work are entirely up to you.

To calculate the annual gross income you hope to achieve, multiply either the day rate by 156 or the hourly rate by 1248. Remember that business expenses, tax and National Insurance (NI) need to be deducted from these amounts to give the net or 'take-home' pay.

Use Table 3.1 to estimate your likely business expenses. This will give you an idea of how much may be deducted from your gross income. To estimate your tax and NI contributions, contact www.hmrc.gov.uk for guidance or discuss it with your accountant.

Remember that this assumes that you can get sufficient work to keep you occupied full time and the rate of pay you hope to achieve could be different than what you are able to achieve. You are more likely to have inconsistent work patterns, being very busy at certain times yet worrying about the lack of work at other times. Your income can vary dramatically from year to year. It is wise to review your income over a period of a few years to assess your true earnings.

Reviewing your rates

Clients never welcome an increase in your fee. Your contract needs to include an annual review of your rates and fee (see Section 6.1). Based on inflation, you may need to alter your established rate. In certain situations you will, of course, need to discuss any change or increase. To avoid re-negotiating face to face or by telephone, inform your clients in writing a month before any changes you consider necessary are due to take place. This allows them time to contact you if they wish to question an alteration. During difficult economic times, I have kept my rate the same or even considered a reduction to keep work.

5 Interview tips

Most interviews for freelance work are reasonably straightforward. Treat each interview as an opportunity to develop your interview techniques and perfect your presentation skills. This will avoid feeling that an interview may have been a waste of your time and travelling expenses, if the work turns out to be unsuitable. The more interviews you attend, the more comfortable you will become. One of the pleasures of working freelance is when an interview is successful and you gain rewarding work opportunities and work with interesting people.

Preparing for an interview

Once you have an interview date booked, it is essential to plan and fully prepare in advance. You will make a much better impression if you have a basic knowledge of the company and its products, so spend some time researching them. Find out what their ranges are like, who they sell to and where they sell. Is it a UK or a foreign company? If you have been sent a brief of the work involved, read and study it thoroughly, making sure you fully understand the requirements. Make notes of any questions you may wish to ask and take them with you to the interview. Take into account the two-way process of an interview: is the work suitable for you?

Ideally, a designer should research my company before meeting me by looking at my website to see the type of clothing that we manufacture. I would expect the designer to have made some sketches to give me an idea of their creativeness.

Heather Benhrima, Kasbah

First impressions are important, so consider carefully what you will wear and dress appropriately. The way you dress is a statement and a selling tool (see Section 2.6).

Plan your journey with care and allow sufficient time to avoid last-minute panics. It does not look good to arrive late and flustered.

Prepare your portfolio in advance. Take a copy of your company profile and CV (see Section 2.4) even if you have sent them to the client already. Remember the name of the interviewer and anyone else involved in the interview. Never leave unpaid-for work with an interviewer (see Section 2.7).

> *When I prepare for interviews, I research the company and their products. I select what I am going to present and prepare an outline of what I intend saying. I like to include colours, fabrics, trends or information for the next season so that companies can see that I am pro-active and forward thinking. Knowing something about competitor ranges is also important.*
>
> Shirley Harrison, Shirley Harrison Fashion Design

During an interview

Remember to switch off your mobile phone before an interview. Give a firm handshake when you arrive and leave; be friendly and approachable even if you feel nervous. Speak clearly and with confidence. Answer questions fully and don't forget to ask questions of your own. Be interested and enthusiastic, but try not to come across as desperate, even if you do happen to be very short of work. Consider your body language, your posture and the way you sit. Make eye contact, smile and show you are listening.

During the interview you may be asked about other projects you have worked on, so be clear about other clients' copyright and confidentiality. You want to reassure the client that if they were to offer you the contract, you would not display examples of their work to other clients or to their competition. It would be unwise to work for two clients in direct competition on the same products at the same time. They would not be happy if they found out and you would very likely lose both as clients.

When discussing the client's requirements, fees, timescales and contracts, be clear and precise. You are unlikely to be able to work out the correct costs in your head during the interview, so don't be tempted to try.

After an interview

Give yourself sufficient time to consider how long the project will actually take and how much the expenses are likely to be, along with any problems, timescales and practical delivery dates. When you are happy with your calculations, confirm in writing the details that were discussed as you understand them, in the form of an estimate or quote within a reasonable timescale (see Section 4.1).

If you feel the work is unsuitable and you really do not want to do it, give yourself time to think and then decline a day or two later. Do not be bullied into accepting unrealistic delivery dates, again, give yourself time to consider if the timescale really is practical (see Section 8.5).

Two employers' points of view

> *I think a good presentation is extremely important. This is easier to do when you have some solid experience behind you, but a strong personality backed up with quality work produced through college training will do just as well. Remember that you are probably one of several people who will be interviewed for the position. You will need to leave your interviewer with a strong reminder of what you are all about and your abilities and why they need to choose you. More importantly, they need to feel that they can work with you. Larger projects will require hours being spent together in the same room. If you don't get on, it could be awkward and extremely hard going for both parties.*
>
> Marcus Cridland, Sales and Marketing Director,
> Shires Equestrian Products

> *The freelance designer I worked with for many years was not my first choice. Her portfolio didn't really give me what I needed. I didn't know if she was capable of designing the type of clothes that I manufactured. I don't think she did much research on me before the interview. She did, however, have a lot of self-confidence, outlined what she thought she could do for my company and I came away thinking that she could perhaps do the job. I decided on another designer and offered her the job. I was delighted with my choice, as this person seemed to have everything that was needed. She had already worked for a similar clothing company, I liked her dress sense and we had got along well at the interview. Unfortunately, she was offered a full-time job and decided to go with that. I decided to call my second choice with a job offer.*
>
> Heather Benhrima, Kasbah

CHAPTER

4

Estimates and Invoices

1 Calculating an estimate or quote

Note: Your estimate or quote is your responsibility; the information included in this book is to be used as a guide only.

It is worth spending sufficient time preparing estimates and fixed quotes. Calculate these as accurately and effectively as you can or it could cost you time and money. Take into account the amount of time a project will take you and the cost of any expenses, such as materials, stationery and travel. Include absolutely everything. You may need to estimate your expenses to some extent, as it can be very difficult to be completely accurate where these are concerned. You may also need to include provision for certain expenses to be paid to you in advance. It is essential to leave a degree of flexibility to ensure you are not out of pocket.

Heather Benhrima of Kasbah was reassured:

> At the negotiation stage, my freelance designer was very precise with regards to contracts, hours worked, expenses, designs, etc. I found this quite daunting to begin with but comforting at the same time. This person knew what she was talking about.

Alterations can often add up to many extra hours' work and, if you do not include them in your calculations, they can eat into your fee. Some clients have a long list, others very few or possibly none. As alterations can be so time-consuming, a percentage in your budget needs to be allowed in order to accommodate them.

Save all letters and emails relating to any work requested and any work you undertake. You may need them as documentary evidence at a later date.

Send estimates or quotes swiftly; don't forget that the client could be receiving several. Send them as soon as you possibly can, within a day or two. Be seen to be organised and efficient. Keeping the client waiting weeks for an estimate or quote is unprofessional and unacceptable; you may very well lose your credibility and the work.

Calculating how long a project will take

It can be difficult to give an accurate estimate, as the requirements of each client are so individual. For example, once you have a 'history' with a client, design and development could be less time-consuming: a garment that has been successful one season may be updated and adapted for the following season. To calculate how long future projects will take, time yourself for each task on which you work and record it in your working diary (see Section 8.2). When starting out, you could set yourself a small project and time yourself carefully to ensure your first estimate or quote is accurate. This could be used as an example of your work and added to your portfolio.

I have timed myself on numerous occasions and worked out a guide for estimating how long a project will take me. I sometimes include examples of my work, in PDF or JPG

Table 4.1   **Design package calculator**

Task	Hours	Cost
Phase 1: Research and design development		
Phase 1: Colour palette (six colours or fewer) – A4 CADS[1] (PDF)		
Phase 2: Colour presentation standard average garment designs showing front and back view, maximum of three colourways – A4 CADS (PDF)		
Phase 2: Full garment detailing – A4 CADS (PDF)		
Phase 3: Size specifications, including illustration and grades, for a maximum of six sizes (PDF)		
Total for six garments		
Divide by six to calculate hours and price per garment		

[1] CADS means 'computer-aided design sheets'.

format, to give a guide to what is involved and illustrate how the work will be presented. I estimate expenses separately to give the client an overall idea of the total costs involved.

Table 4.1 shows an example of a basic design package calculator for six garments. For fewer than six garments, you would need to allow extra time for each item. See Section 11.2 for phases of a design project.

Any computer files sent to a client must be in a fixed format (PDF or JPG) to prevent alterations and to preserve your intellectual property rights (see Section 6.3).

> ‘ My proposal includes a breakdown of all the work involved, exactly what the client will receive and the estimated costs. I like to start the design process by creating trend, colour or influence boards relating to the products that are being developed. I use the boards as visual aids as they encourage discussion and maintain focus.’
>
> Shirley Harrison, Shirley Harrison Fashion Design

Providing a fixed fee quote

A fixed fee quote is a fixed price for an entire project within an agreed timescale, excluding expenses. Make sure the client understands that only the work within the quote will be undertaken for the agreed price. Confirm in writing, but include provision to cover additional work, such as alterations, as an extra cost at your hourly rate. Include a separate estimate for the cost of any expenses likely to be incurred. Confirm that the client understands the expenses are approximate, not a fixed sum like the quote for the work (see Sections 3.4 and 4.3).

Providing an estimate based on an hourly rate

Rates an hour can be how you work a job out but not quoted to a client until you begin working for them. If you do choose this method state your hourly rate and the number of hours you estimate that the work in question will take. Give an approximate total price and timescale. It is not possible to fix a price when working this way but it needs to be reasonably accurate. Some clients much prefer this method of working as it gives them greater flexibility, especially with alterations. Confirm your estimate in writing with a separate estimate of expenses likely to be incurred. Ensure the client understands that it is an estimate for the work and expenses involved – not a fixed sum. If the client asks for a considerable amount of extra work to be completed, far more than the original estimate, discuss it fully before continuing and confirm with a second written estimate to avoid any misunderstandings. This type of agreement is not suitable for clients with a tight or fixed budget.

Providing an estimate based on a season rate

A 'season rate' is an agreed fee for a fixed number of hours to be worked within a six-month period for Spring/Summer or Autumn/Winter and has the advantage of confirming the amount of work and income for six months. Dates, exact hours to be worked and timescales need to be agreed. Confirm these in writing stating your terms, including provision to cover any additional work you may be asked to complete, such as alterations. This should be agreed by both parties. Make sure the client understands that it is only the hours within the quote that will be undertaken for the agreed price. Include a separate written estimate for the cost of expenses likely to be incurred. Confirm that the client understands that they are approximate, not a fixed sum like the fee for the work, and need to be reimbursed on top of the agreed fee.

One of my clients had a budget we worked to each season and reviewed annually. This took into account travelling abroad and working in the UK. Initially, I invoiced a third of the total amount pro-forma. I then sent a second invoice about halfway through the project and a final invoice on completion. All payments were due by return. I later tried monthly payments directly into my bank account. Each method had its benefits. Any extra hours above those agreed I charged for; requesting a cheque by return along with expenses incurred. This was written into my estimate, agreed and then confirmed in my six-month contract.

Details to include on estimates and quotes

Your estimates or quotes should be written in a clear legible font and include the following details:

- your business heading address, telephone numbers and email addresses;
- your client's full name, company name, business address, telephone numbers and email addresses;
- the date;

- a title, i.e. 'Estimate' or 'Quote';
- the exact work involved and included in the price;
- the format in which all work will be sent (i.e. PDF or JPG files);
- how much you are to be paid for the work (e.g. an hourly or daily rate);
- an estimate of the expenses;
- payment terms;
- whether or not you are registered for VAT;
- a statement that any extra work will be charged at your hourly rate;
- the agreed place of work;
- a statement of who owns what and when (a 'retention of title' clause could protect your designs and copyright and encourage prompt payment (see Sections 6.1 and 6.2));
- a statement that the next stage is to agree and confirm all details in a written contract if the estimate or quote is acceptable.

For speed and ease, compile yourself a template for estimates and quotes. You could divide the work into phases as a guide to timescales and prices. The phases could be linked to your payment terms.

2 Invoicing clients

Note: Your invoice is your responsibility; the information included in this book is to be used as a guide only.

Send completed work by a secure method that requires a signature for goods on arrival if you are not delivering personally. This gives proof of arrival and confirmation of the date received. When sending work by email, you must confirm that your client has received it all. Ask them for written confirmation that all your work has arrived.

Invoice your clients promptly at the agreed intervals and on completion of work. If you are paid on a monthly basis, submit your invoice a few days before the agreed deadline to ensure your client receives it in sufficient time. The most common date for submission is the last day of the month. This avoids waiting an extra month for your money.

Invoices need to be clear and accurate to avoid delays in payment, and this will aid cash flow. It is essential that your invoices are correct; double-check your calculations to confirm.

You may prefer to post your invoice; if you email it, send it in PDF or JPG format for security, to prevent alterations.

Creating an invoice

Your invoices should be written in a clear legible font and include the following details:

- your business heading address, telephone numbers and email addresses;
- your client's full name, company name, business address, telephone numbers and email addresses;

- the date;
- a title, i.e. 'Invoice';
- a unique invoice number – for easy reference, you might number them for individual clients, e.g. XYZ001, XYZ002;
- a description of the work (tasks undertaken), including hours worked, rate agreed and total price (see Table 4.1);
- itemised expenses;
- sub total;
- if VAT registered, your VAT registration number, VAT percentage and amount;
- total amount due;
- payment terms, i.e. 'due by return';
- method of payment, i.e. cheque or BACS payment;
- details of who a cheque is to be made payable to or bank account details.

See www.hmrc.gov.uk for additional information to be included on invoices if you are registered for VAT.

Expenses should be itemised on a pre-prepared invoice and updated regularly, saving time and avoiding the possibility of missing out expenses. A separate Excel chart that totals expenses is an easy option.

Writing a template invoice

Compile an invoice template (see Table 4.2) for speed and ease. Write your own using a template from your computer software as a starting point or browse the Internet for ideas. An Excel template invoice is an easy option that can automatically add up the numbers for you.

Receiving payment

Keep a copy of every invoice. Note on the copy when the invoice is paid, the method of payment and the account it was paid into; for example, you might write 'paid in full by cheque' and the date you paid it into your account.

Table 4.2 Invoice template

Design work for .... range .... hours @ £..........	= £..........
Alterations for .... range .... hours @ £..........	= £..........
Total expenses (see itemised list attached)	= £..........
Sub total	= £..........
VAT @ 20%	= £..........
Total due	= £..........

If only part of an invoice is paid, write the amount that has been paid, the date paid, the method of payment and the account paid into. You need to address immediately the issue of why full payment has not been made.

3 Travelling abroad with and for a client

Be clear from the beginning that your client will be paying for all your travel costs, subsistence and any other reasonable expenses while you are travelling abroad on their behalf, and confirm this in your letter of confirmation or contract. The client should always book and pay for your flights and hotels (after agreeing timings and itinerary with you in advance). Do not pay for them yourself and expect to be reimbursed. You should have a room to yourself: it is not reasonable to be asked to share. Ensure you have the correct paperwork to prove your hotel and flights have been booked and paid well in advance of your journey. Draw up a schedule of likely expenses and request funds in advance to cover expenses you anticipate (see Section 8.5).

Be quite specific from an early stage in your discussions with your client about the hours you will charge for when travelling abroad. This avoids the possibility of working unreasonable and excessive hours when travelling for or with them. A common issue is travelling to a foreign trade show 'for the day': it usually takes more hours than an average working day. Make it very clear that you are not prepared to work a 24-hour day and be paid for only eight hours (see Section 8.5). You may need to include an overnight stay or be away for longer, anything from a few days to a week or more. It is therefore reasonable to charge for travelling time and hours worked. Your client is buying your time: while travelling for them you are unable to work for another client. Remember to take into account time differences between countries when making your calculations.

If you do agree to take the earliest flight out and return on the latest flight back on the day of a trip, make it clear that the client pays for the total number of hours involved including all travelling time and any delays.

Accommodation for early starts or late arrivals

For a very early departure from an airport a considerable distance away from your home, it is reasonable that your client pays for you to stay in an airport hotel. The same applies to late night or early morning arrivals. It is not reasonable or safe for you to be expected to wait for hours during the night or early hours of the morning to catch a train home. The client should pay for a taxi or an airport hotel.

Travel delays

Travelling time, including delays, should be charged at your hourly rate. You and your client need to come to an agreement about your fees if this happens. Although it is reasonable for you to expect full payment to cover those hours, it may be wiser to compromise and come to a mutual agreement. Any extra hotel fees, fares and subsistence incurred due to a delay should be charged as an extra and paid for by your client. This must all be outlined and confirmed in your letter of confirmation or contract.

I often encounter delays while travelling; most only last an hour or so, fortunately. On one occasion, my client and I were booked on the last flight of the day back to the UK, which was eventually cancelled at midnight after waiting several hours. Chaos ensued; we were informed that replacement flights could take up to several days. As we were unable to book another flight or airport hotel, we travelled to the station to wait for the first train home. We ended up at 3 A.M. in an all-night bar opposite the station along with other passengers from the same flight. I remember one passenger saying that he had left his car in the one-day parking, which was very expensive. We were so tired and fed-up by this time, we decided to book into a nearby hotel (an extra cost to my client) that still had a few rooms available.

We returned home by train (another extra cost to my client) later the next day and were collected by my partner, who drove for an hour and a half to collect us (a cost to my partner). The train was expensive due to travelling at the last minute but we found that return tickets were slightly cheaper! We did manage to work during the journey home. In the end, we compromised regarding my payment for the extra time involved.

4 What your client expects from you

Your client expects competence and professionalism from you. They are employing you for your knowledge and expertise. They may look to you for advice and guidance on issues within the context of your work, and your attitude towards a project speaks volumes. Failure to complete a project within the agreed timescale or to an acceptable standard may well result in complaints and the possibility of the client refusing to pay.

Be polite at all times even in the event of disagreements. You may need to take a step back from a situation to consider how to tackle it. Your client would be very unimpressed if you were to be rude, shout or be off-hand with them even if they or a situation should become difficult. Be very diplomatic at all times.

Try to be available for any reasonable contact from your client. This is helpful should your client encounter a major problem and need your advice. However, it does not mean that you should make a doormat of yourself, work unsociable hours or accept unnecessary calls at inconvenient or unreasonable times.

One of my clients emailed me to thank me for working very hard over a weekend once to resolve a problem for a factory. It was not that convenient for me at the time, but they really appreciated the help.

You may be required to guide your clients with selections for colour prediction and styling or similar. They will expect you to be up to date with your information and predictions. Throughout the course of a working relationship, you could be asked to give suggestions and recommendations for the work in question. Some clients know exactly what they want you to do, others may ask for your advice and ideas.

Be sensible in the choice of work that you accept. If asked to work in an area in which you have no experience or with which you are uncomfortable, it would be wise to decline, rather than end up in a mess with an unacceptable standard of work. As freelance designers are often expected to be experts in many different areas, this can sometimes lead to difficulties. For example, some designers are happy to work on size charts and grading as well as design and development; others are not. Some like to cut first patterns; others do not. In some instances, it would be wise to sub-contract to an expert in the required field but ensure that there are sufficient funds within the project budget to cover the costs.

CHAPTER 5

Financial Matters

1 Choosing an accountant

A good accountant is an asset. Handling your accounts yourself can save money in fees but you may not be aware of all the benefits you could claim and it will take time.

> ❝Most accountants will be happy to give a quote, before undertaking the work, once they know exactly what is involved and this can be helpful from a budgeting perspective.❞
>
> Alison, tax advisor

When choosing an accountant, ask for recommendations and make enquiries with several to compare services and annual cost. A self-employed accountant can be worth considering. My accountant lives 50 miles away but has other clients in my area, making meetings easy. He is efficient, easy to contact and also self-employed, which makes his rates competitive.

Shirley Harrison of Shirley Harrison Fashion Design uses a different method:

> When I started working freelance, I used an accountant for many years. When I moved to a new county, I continued using her by posting the information. This worked for a while until I was unable to keep up with her timetable.
>
> Currently, I collect all my accounting information (invoices, expenses, receipts and bills for running costs) and then hand them over to my husband who uses an accounting software package to work out the profit and loss sheet and a breakdown of costs. Previously, these figures were collected and presented to the accountant who would audit the accounts, calculate my tax and also notify the Inland Revenue on my behalf.
>
> My husband continues to use accounting software for my accounts and gets the correct information from the HMRC website for direction on allowable expenses. These are expenses directly used in the business, for example, a proportion of house expenses (such as, light, heat, telephone and Internet but not rent), capital equipment (computers, drawing boards, etc.), travel and car expenses (mileage).
>
> I keep records of all income and expenditure. I have to be able to justify all claims if challenged by the Inland Revenue.

If you decide to register and trade as a limited company, you are strongly advised to employ an accountant, as Wendy Burns of Wendy Burns Designs Ltd discovered:

After 12 years establishing myself as a freelance textile designer (sole trader) for retail, suppliers and manufacturers, a retailer I was working for on a regular basis capped the amount I could earn, but informed me this could change if I were to go limited – a rather daunting thought at first but relatively straight-forward. This required me to look for a new accountant, register my company and open a business account. The key is to find a good accountant; luckily I have. I now pay myself a regular salary, pension and life insurance through my company. What has been difficult is realising the business account is not mine. I have the benefit of being a director (I don't think that would have ever happened to me in my industry) but I am an employee of the company. A posi-tive is that if I were to be sued it would be the company and not myself as an individual; something worth considering if you are a sole trader. Some fellow freelancers take out an additional indemnity insurance to cover themselves against being sued.

Alison, a tax advisor, says:

There are advantages and disadvantages to incorporating and your account-ant will be able to advise you. A limited company can add kudos, mitigate the commercial risk and be cheaper for tax and NIC if profits rise and are reinvested in the business, but the administrative burden is considerably higher and there is less privacy as business results are available in the public domain.

2 Finance and bank accounts

If you have no savings with which to start your business, consider other options such as a loan or the possibility of a grant. For example, if you are under 25 years' old, the Prince's Trust could be worth contacting or try a professional organisation for informa-tion on funding. I didn't borrow money to start my freelance business. I used savings and I reinvest some of my earnings when necessary. That way it avoids the worry and expense of paying back a loan.

If you decide a loan is the only option, consider the number of years, payment terms, interest rates and monthly payments. Thoroughly check the small print and details of individual loans for extra fees, charges or restrictions that may apply. One that allows early repayment could be an advantage.

> *If your loan meets the 'wholly and exclusively for business purposes' test, the interest will be deductible for tax.*
>
> Alison, tax advisor

It can be difficult to balance repaying a loan whilst saving for tax, VAT and covering your day-to-day living costs. Do not make the mistake of spending your tax and VAT money – you will just end up in a terrible financial mess. Budget very carefully; do not spend money you do not have. There may be a suitable bank account available enabling you to control your income, your expenditure and your loan more effectively. If you find yourself earning good money, it may be advisable to pay off your loan sooner rather than later. Save some of your spare cash for the future when work is scarce; think ahead and budget.

If you use a credit card, pay it in full each month to avoid debt building up. Avoid paying by card if you find it difficult to control your finances.

Consider the types of bank account available and investigate your options before making decisions. Check all details including interest rates, fees and the small print. Consider location: a local branch and an Internet-based account? Linked Internet current and savings accounts enable ease of use and have the added bonus of interest. A third account to save for tax and VAT may be helpful. Double-check that any account you choose is suitable for you to use for your business.

It is essential that you keep all finance details, bank and credit card statements – personal and business – for your books.

3 Income tax

It is very important to register as self-employed with HM Revenue & Customs (HMRC) as soon as you begin self-employment. If you cease to be self-employed, you need to submit your final Self-Assessment Return for that year stating the date you stopped trading.

It is mandatory to file an annual Self-Assessment Return while self-employed. You can complete it yourself. If you complete it online, your tax is calculated for you. Alternatively your accountant can complete a return on your behalf and notify you how much tax you will need to pay and when to pay it. There is a deadline for submission; you face a fine if you fail to meet the deadline. You will receive a Self-Assessment Statement for tax from HM Revenue & Customs showing all your transactions.

> *HMRC have recently updated their penalty system. Late filing penalties are now harsher than they used to be and they are payable even if no tax is due. Interest is payable on tax paid after the due date.*
>
> Alison, tax advisor

The UK tax year starts on 6 April. You are required to pay tax for the previous tax year before a deadline of 31 January plus a calculated percentage, based on your previous year's earnings, towards your next year's tax (known as a 'payment on account'). A second 'payment on account' is due before 31 July for the next tax year. If you fail to meet these deadlines, you face a penalty.

For example, imagine that it's 1 January 2012. By 31 January 2012, you need to have paid in full your tax for the tax year 2010–11 (which ended on 5 April 2011). You also need to pay your first payment on account for the tax year 2011–12. A second payment on account is due by 31 July 2012. These two payments are based on your earnings during the tax year 2010–11.

If you earn substantially less during the next tax year, you should contact HM Revenue & Customs to reduce your payments on account based on the figures that you estimate your earnings will be. If your income is low you may be able to claim tax credits.

Contact HM Revenue & Customs or Business Link for further information.

4 Bookkeeping and accountancy

You need to keep your books (accounts) for the number of years specified by HM Revenue & Customs.

> *You may be required to produce your business paperwork to HM Revenue & Customs in the event of an enquiry.*
>
> Alison, tax advisor

It is imperative that you keep accurate records of all your income and expenditure. As a guide keep all sales and purchase invoices, expenses receipts plus bank records and statements. Your accountant can guide you on the information you need to record and keep or you may consult HM Revenue & Customs yourself.

Dates for your annual accounts

Your first year's books may run for longer than a year. You need to decide a date on which to base your annual accounts. The financial or tax year runs from 6 April to 5 April. The most common dates for accounts are from 1 April to 31 March: it is usual to finish at the end of the month.

> ❛ *If you are a sole trader and it is convenient for you to adopt a 31st March or 5th April year end, this will be the most straightforward for tax purposes.* ❜
>
> Alison, tax advisor

Allowances and expenses deducted from taxable income

Allowances and expenses can be rather complex and confusing, especially for people working from home, when a percentage of certain expenses may need to be calculated. An accountant can advise on these issues (or contact HM Revenue & Customs for information). If you are working from home and you claim part of your house is used exclusively for business, you could be liable for business rates or capital gains tax.

The following list gives a summary of allowances and expenses:

- Personal allowance is the amount of money you are allowed to earn each year before tax; it usually changes each year.
- Allowances are costs that you are allowed to offset against your business takings.
- Capital allowances include, for example, equipment for your business.
- Business expenses include, for example, travelling expenses to a trade show.
- Private expenses are not allowed to be offset against your business takings.

Recording all your information on a regular basis makes it easier to complete your Self-Assessment Return at the end of the tax year and avoids last-minute panic.

An easy way to record your business transactions is to use an Excel spreadsheet. Once set up, the charts can calculate the totals. You can create your own income and expenditure charts using the example templates that accompany this book as a guide even if you plan to use an accountant. (The more you can do yourself, the less you need to pay your accountant.) Be sure to check and double-check that the charts you use are working correctly.

Use one worksheet for the whole tax year, adding more rows if needed, or use multiple worksheets in the same document. Use separate documents for income and expenditure to avoid confusion.

Note: It is important to familiarise yourself with the charts and how they work. Download an example chart and experiment with it to see how it works. If you find it difficult to understand, read the Excel instruction manual or consider taking a course in Excel.

Income chart

Download the Income Template spreadsheet (see Figure 5.1) from the book's website and re-name it. Open your spreadsheet. It consists of two worksheets: EXAMPLE is for

NAME: J. Smith

INCOME

TAX YEAR: 6th April 2010 to 5th April 2011

NO	DATE	INVOICE NO	CLIENT	DESIGN FEES	MATERIALS	STATIONERY	POSTAGE	TELEPHONE	TRAVEL/ACCOM	SUNDRIES	TOTALS	Date paid
1	1-May-10	XYZ001	XYZ Designs Ltd	£ 2,000.00		£ 50.00	£ 10.00				£ 2,060.00	31-May-10
2											£ 0.00	
3											£ 0.00	
4											£ 0.00	
5											£ 0.00	
6											£ 0.00	
7											£ 0.00	
8											£ 0.00	
9											£ 0.00	
10											£ 0.00	
11											£ 0.00	
12											£ 0.00	
13											£ 0.00	
14											£ 0.00	
15											£ 0.00	
16											£ 0.00	
17											£ 0.00	
18											£ 0.00	
19											£ 0.00	
20											£ 0.00	
21											£ 0.00	
22											£ 0.00	
23											£ 0.00	
24											£ 0.00	
25											£ 0.00	
26											£ 0.00	
27											£ 0.00	
28											£ 0.00	
29											£ 0.00	
30											£ 0.00	
NO	DATE	INVOICE NO	CLIENT	DESIGN FEES	MATERIALS	STATIONERY	POSTAGE	TELEPHONE	TRAVEL/ACCOM	SUNDRIES	TOTALS	Date paid
TOTALS				£ 2,000.00	£ 0.00	£ 50.00	£ 10.00	£ 0.00	£ 0.00	£ 0.00	£ 2,060.00	
										TOTALS	£ 2,060.00	

This chart is to be used as a guide only. Any similarity to any other chart is coincidental. The author and publisher do not accept any liability.

Figure 5.1 Income Template spreadsheet

you to experiment with; INCOME is ready for you to use. Click on EXAMPLE or INCOME at the bottom left to view the worksheet.

To prepare your worksheet, enter the following information into the correct cells:

- your name;
- the tax year.

Enter the categories of income you need to record in the shaded cells running across the sheet in row 3 and row 34 (e.g. materials, stationery).

If you need more categories of income, you can add columns to the worksheet. Select the Insert option from the menu and click Columns. You need to add the formulas to any new columns, so it may be simpler to copy and paste an empty column that contains the formulas. Then double-check all formulas in the worksheet.

To enter income and use your chart, enter the following information into one row per invoice:

- date of invoice;
- invoice number;
- client;
- design fees and any other items on the invoice.

When you enter an amount, you do not need to use the '£' sign; just enter the numbers, such as 2000 or 42.5 The chart will add the '£' sign and pennies to give £2000.00 or £42.50. When a payment is made, you can add the date to the appropriate row (in column M).

Your downloaded worksheet calculates column and row totals. Cells L34 and L35 should show exactly the same total. If they do not, re-check your chart formulas (see Figure 5.2). When you click on a cell, its formula shows in the formula bar. Make corrections in the formula bar, not in the cell. Check your chart to ensure that it is calculating correctly.

To add rows to the worksheet, select the Insert option from the menu and click Rows. You need to add the formulas to any new rows, so it may be simpler to copy and paste an empty row that contains the formulas. Then double-check all formulas in the worksheet.

To add more worksheets to the document, select the Insert option from the menu and click Worksheet. You can then copy and paste your existing worksheet to the new worksheet and double-check all formulas.

Remember: Double-check your charts to ensure they are calculating correctly each time you use them. Use Figure 5.2 as a guide to the correct formulas and cell formats to ensure that they are working correctly.

Expenditure chart

Download the Expenditure Template spreadsheet (see Figure 5.3) from the book's website and re-name it. Open your spreadsheet. It consists of 14 worksheets: EXAMPLE is

NAME:												
TAX YEAR:	6th April ...... (year) to 5th April ...... (year)					INCOME						
NO	DATE	INVOICE NO	CLIENT	DESIGN FEES	MATERIALS	STATIONERY	POSTAGE	TELEPHONE	TRAVEL/ACCOM	SUNDRIES	TOTALS	Date paid
1											=SUM(E4:K4)	
2											=SUM(E5:K5)	
3											=SUM(E6:K6)	
4											=SUM(E7:K7)	
5											=SUM(E8:K8)	
6											=SUM(E9:K9)	
7											=SUM(E10:K10)	
8											=SUM(E11:K11)	
9											=SUM(E12:K12)	
10											=SUM(E13:K13)	
11											=SUM(E14:K14)	
12											=SUM(E15:K15)	
13											=SUM(E16:K16)	
14											=SUM(E17:K17)	
15											=SUM(E18:K18)	
16											=SUM(E19:K19)	
17											=SUM(E20:K20)	
18											=SUM(E21:K21)	
19											=SUM(E22:K22)	
20											=SUM(E23:K23)	
21											=SUM(E24:K24)	
22											=SUM(E25:K25)	
23											=SUM(E26:K26)	
24											=SUM(E27:K27)	
25											=SUM(E28:K28)	
26											=SUM(E29:K29)	
27											=SUM(E30:K30)	
28											=SUM(E31:K31)	
29											=SUM(E32:K32)	
30											=SUM(E33:K33)	
NO	DATE	INVOICE NO	CLIENT	DESIGN FEES	MATERIALS	STATIONERY	POSTAGE	TELEPHONE	TRAVEL/ACCOM	SUNDRIES	**=SUM(L4:L33)**	
TOTALS				=SUM(E4:E33)	=SUM(F4:F33)	=SUM(G4:G33)	=SUM(H4:H33)	=SUM(I4:I33)	=SUM(J4:J33)	=SUM(K4:K33)	**=SUM(E37:K37)**	
				DESIGN FEES	MATERIALS	STATIONERY	POSTAGE	TELEPHONE	TRAVEL/ACCOM	SUNDRIES	TOTALS	

This chart is to be used as a guide only. Any similarity to any other chart is coincidental. The author and publisher do not accept any liability.

LEGEND:

format cells = general
format cells = general

format cells = date
format cells = custom = "£"#,##0.00;-"£"#,##0.00

Figure 5.2 Income Template formulas

NAME: J Smith
MONTH: May
YEAR: 2010
TAX YEAR: 6th April 2010 to 5th April 2011

EXPENDITURE

DATE	Location	MATERIALS	STATIONERY	POSTAGE	TELEPHONE	TRAVEL/ACCOM	?	?	SUNDRIES	Cost
1	Office Supplies		£ 17.50		£ 20.00					£ 37.50
2	Post Office			£ 5.25						£ 5.25
3										£ 0.00
4										£ 0.00
5										£ 0.00
6										£ 0.00
7										£ 0.00
8										£ 0.00
9										£ 0.00
10										£ 0.00
11										£ 0.00
12										£ 0.00
13										£ 0.00
14										£ 0.00
15										£ 0.00
16										£ 0.00
17										£ 0.00
18										£ 0.00
19										£ 0.00
20										£ 0.00
21										£ 0.00
22										£ 0.00
23										£ 0.00
24										£ 0.00
25										£ 0.00
26										£ 0.00
27										£ 0.00
28										£ 0.00
29										£ 0.00
30										£ 0.00
31										£ 0.00
DATE	Location	MATERIALS	STATIONERY	POSTAGE	TELEPHONE	TRAVEL/ACCOM	?	?	SUNDRIES	
TOTALS		£ 0.00	£ 17.50	£ 5.25	£ 20.00	£ 0.00	£ 0.00	£ 0.00	£ 0.00	£ 42.75
										£ 42.75
										TOTALS

This chart is to be used as a guide only. Any similarity to any other chart is coincidental. The author and publisher do not accept any liability.

Figure 5.3 Expenditure Template spreadsheet

a worksheet for you to experiment with; the other 13 worksheets are prepared ready for you to use for 12 months' books for one tax year. Click on EXAMPLE or a month at the bottom to view the worksheet.

To prepare each worksheet, enter the following information into the correct cells:

- your name;
- the month;
- the year;
- tax year.

Enter the categories of expenditure you need to record in the shaded cells running across the sheet in row 5 and row 37 (e.g. materials, stationery).

If you need more categories of expenditure, you can add columns to the worksheet. Select the Insert option from the menu and click Columns. You need to add the formulas to any new columns, so it may be simpler to copy and paste an empty column that contains the formulas. Then double-check all formulas in the worksheet.

First, group together all expenditure invoices for each date. If you have more than one invoice for one cell, add them together and enter the total into the cell. For example, if you have three invoices all dated 1 May 2012 for stationery for £10.20, £2.05 and £5.25, they total £17.50. You would therefore enter £17.50 into the Stationery cell for that date i.e. cell D6.

To enter items of expenditure and use your chart, enter the information into one row per date:

- the location where you spent the money e.g. Post Office (if there is more than one entry for that date just select one location);
- the amount of the invoice or receipt; if an invoice has other items that you are not including, highlight the items you do include or make a note on the invoice.

When you enter an amount in a cell, you do not need to use the '£' sign; just enter the numbers, such as 2000 or 42.5 The chart will add the '£' sign and pennies to give £2000.00 or £42.50.

Your downloaded worksheet calculates column and row totals. Cells K37 and K38 should show exactly the same total. If they do not, re-check your chart formulas (see Figure 5.4). When you click on a cell, its formula shows in the formula bar. Make corrections in the formula bar, not in the cell. Check your chart to ensure that it is calculating correctly.

Remember: Double-check your charts to ensure they are calculating correctly each time you use them. Use Figure 5.4 as a guide to the correct formulas and cell formats to ensure that they are working correctly.

NAME:	J Smith									
MONTH:	May		EXPENDITURE							
YEAR:	2010									
TAX YEAR:	6th April 2010 to 5th April 2011									
DATE	Location	MATERIALS	STATIONERY	POSTAGE	TELEPHONE	TRAVEL/ACCOM	?	?	SUNDRIES	Cost
1										=SUM(C6:J6)
2										=SUM(C7:J7)
3										=SUM(C8:J8)
4										=SUM(C9:J9)
5										=SUM(C10:J10)
6										=SUM(C11:J11)
7										=SUM(C12:J12)
8										=SUM(C13:J13)
9										=SUM(C14:J14)
10										=SUM(C15:J15)
11										=SUM(C16:J16)
12										=SUM(C17:J17)
13										=SUM(C18:J18)
14										=SUM(C19:J19)
15										=SUM(C20:J20)
16										=SUM(C21:J21)
17										=SUM(C22:J22)
18										=SUM(C23:J23)
19										=SUM(C24:J24)
20										=SUM(C25:J25)
21										=SUM(C26:J26)
22										=SUM(C27:J27)
23										=SUM(C28:J28)
28										=SUM(C33:J33)
29										=SUM(C34:J34)
30										=SUM(C35:J35)
31										=SUM(C36:J36)
DATE	Location	MATERIALS	STATIONERY	POSTAGE	TELEPHONE	TRAVEL/ACCOM	?	?	SUNDRIES	
TOTALS		=SUM(C6:C36)	=SUM(D6:D36)	=SUM(E6:E36)	=SUM(F6:F36)	=SUM(G6:G36)	=SUM(H6:H36)	=SUM(I6:I37)	=SUM(J6:J37)	=SUM(K6:K36)
									TOTALS	=SUM(C38:J38)

This chart is to be used as a guide only. Any similarity to any other chart is coincidental. The author and publisher do not accept any liability.

LEGEND:

format cells = general
format cells = general

format cells = custom = "£"#,##0.00;-"£"#,##0.00

Figure 5.4 Expenditure Template formulas

5 National Insurance contributions

You must pay Class 2 National Insurance contributions (NICs) to keep yourself covered for the benefits they provide or you risk a fine, unless your earnings are below the small earnings threshold. If your earnings do fall below the threshold, you can apply for Small Earnings Exception (SEE).

Class 4 NICs are payable in addition to Class 2 NICs if your business profit is over a limit specified by HM Revenue & Customs. The percentage is calculated with your tax and fluctuates with your earnings. It is possible in some situations to pay too much NICs. If you think you have overpaid, contact your accountant or HM Revenue & Customs.

> *There can be time limits for reclaiming NICs and tax, so don't delay. Details can be found on the HMRC website or by calling their helpline.*
>
> Alison, tax advisor

6 VAT – do I need to register?

Value added tax (VAT) is subject to change and has different rates that apply to different items. If your business turnover exceeds the VAT threshold, you need to register. It may be to your advantage to register even if you do not exceed the threshold, as you would then be able to claim back much of the VAT you pay out. If you do register, you need to charge VAT on all your invoices and complete VAT returns. There are different methods of paying VAT. The Flat Rate Scheme is worth considering as it may be an easier, simpler option for you and can be less time-consuming.

VAT is not as complicated as it may initially seem; you should get used to the process relatively quickly. Either pay your accountant to deal with your VAT returns or complete them yourself. This can be done online, which can give a few extra days to pay.

> *There are deadlines for registering for VAT and penalties if you notify late. Keep an eye on the level of your turnover and inform HMRC straight away if you reach the threshold.*
>
> Alison, tax advisor

7 Pension provision

Retirement may seem a long way off, but you really do need to consider your options now. Estimate the state pension you will get by obtaining a 'State Pension Forecast' and calculate how much money you are likely to need to live on when you retire. This will help you decide the amount of extra provision you will need in order to have sufficient income during your old age.

As a self-employed person paying Class 2 NICs, you will only be entitled to a basic state pension. This is less than someone in full-time employment paying the higher rate Class 1 NICs.

A personal pension plan is well worth considering. There are several different types and you need to spend time investigating them. Working on a freelance basis can make your earnings erratic, so consider how much you can realistically afford to pay and check if you qualify for any tax relief on pension contributions. It is wise to reassess your pension needs regularly and increase your contributions if you feel you have underestimated. Shop around and seek professional advice to find a pension that suits your requirements.

> *Tax relief is available on contributions up to the level of your earnings or £50,000 per annum if this is higher. A good Independent Financial Adviser will be able to shop around for you and get the best deal.*
>
> Alison, tax advisor

8 Employing staff

You need to investigate your responsibilities as an employer and check the employment laws for employing on a temporary or permanent basis. Contact your accountant for advice or consult HM Revenue & Customs for information.

> *From a tax point of view, employers are obliged to operate a PAYE scheme and deduct tax and NIC on behalf of HMRC. A bookkeeper will be able to look after this and might be cheaper than an accountant.*
>
> Alison, tax advisor

As an alternative to employing someone yourself you could ask another self-employed freelancer working from their premises to help you. They could invoice you for the hours they work and you simply pay their invoice. Invoices and payments both need to be included in your books. If they work from your premises, you need to comply with health and safety laws and have the necessary insurance.

9 Health and safety

Ensure that your business premises (and those of your client, if you plan to work there) comply with health and safety and first aid standards. Contact the Health & Safety Executive (HSE) for more information.

10 Insurance

You need to consider what insurance you need while self-employed. Individual policies need to be read and details carefully checked for suitability and confirmation of exactly what is covered. Some are essential; others depend on personal choice and your circumstances.

- Buildings and Contents insurance: If you plan to work from home, check your existing insurance policy to see if you are covered. Extra cover or a separate policy for your business may be needed. Ensure items such as laptops are adequately covered.
- Professional Indemnity insurance: It is wise to cover yourself against the risk of being sued by a client.
- Public Liability insurance: If a client were injured while on your premises and then sued you, public liability insurance would cover you.
- Car insurance: Check your policy covers you to use your car for your freelance work.
- Life insurance: It is wise to cover yourself if you have dependants.
- Income Protection insurance: It is wise to cover yourself for illness and being unable to work for a period of time or permanently.
- Accident and Illness insurance: Check to see exactly what is covered and the timescales of any payments due in the event of a claim.

You can also purchase insurance to cover costs if you were to be investigated by HM Revenue & Customs.

> ‘ *Ask your accountant if he or she operates an 'Enquiry Insurance' scheme if you are concerned about the professional fees that will be involved in the event of an HMRC enquiry.* ’
>
> Alison, tax advisor

CHAPTER 6

Legal Aspects

1 The importance of contracts

Having a contract between yourself and a client is the most professional way of working. It means both parties are clear and understand all of the work involved, including exactly what is to be delivered and when. It is much easier to seek legal help if there is documentary evidence of an agreement.

Always have a written contract signed by both parties, the terms and conditions confirming exactly what has been agreed. It is contractually binding and can avoid later disputes. It is never advisable to work with a company that is not prepared to work with a written contract; its value cannot be underestimated. A written contract reduces the possibility of having to take a company to court. Be wary of a company that tries to alter your contract. Seek the advice of a contract law solicitor before considering any alterations; they may not be in your interest.

Remember a contract works both ways; you must honour your side of the agreement, including completing work on or before the specified date.

> *In my many years' experience in acting for designers, by far the most common reason that they pick up the phone to me is that they have a contractual dispute, usually relating to getting paid. The first question that I always ask is, 'Did they sign your terms and conditions?'*
>
> Tim O'Callaghan, Solicitor, Arnold Fooks Chadwick LLP

2 Writing a contract

Note: Your contract is your responsibility; the information included in this book is to be used as a guide only.

As contract law is such a complicated area, it is advisable to consult a firm that specialises in contract law for the fashion industry. It may seem expensive but paying them to draft your template contract is money well spent. Think of it as an investment for your future security and peace of mind. A great deal of time, expense and anxiety is involved in preparing for court proceedings when a client fails to pay. A professional organisation (see Section 3.2) may be able to recommend an appropriate solicitor.

> *My contract was written for me by a solicitor. On one occasion I used it to get money owed to me when I ended up with two outstanding invoices. In my contract, it said that the copyright would not be handed over until all my invoices were paid. The company was unable to sell the garments until the outstanding invoices were paid.*
>
> Anonymous designer

If you prefer to compile a template contract yourself, do some research first. Be clear and accurate; use straightforward wording and a clear legible font and get it checked over by a contract lawyer before you actually use it. You will usually be charged less if you just ask a solicitor to review a document.

Your contract should include the following details:

- your business heading, company or trading name, address, telephone numbers and email addresses;
- client's company/trading name, business address, telephone numbers and email addresses;
- date;
- title, e.g. 'Contract';
- names of both parties;
- who is employing whom;
- confirmation that your client has the authority and is in a position to enter into a legal contract;
- a statement that the most recent contract replaces all previous discussions and correspondence;
- the exact work you are employed to complete;
- a statement that all work will be sent in PDF, JPG or similar fixed file format, or as hard copies, original artwork, printouts of 'x' number of designs with front and back views in A4 or A3, colour or black and white;
- how much you are to be paid for the work (the hourly or daily rate or a project price);
- a statement that any extra work required will be charged as an extra at your hourly rate;
- a statement of who is responsible for payment of, e.g. expenses for foreign travel;
- the agreed sum to be paid in advance to cover any expenses likely to accrue;
- commencement and completion dates or guidelines;
- a statement that you cannot be responsible for late deadlines if the client has been late in signing off work or selecting at any stage;
- the agreed place of work;
- a 'retention of title' clause that states all work remains your property until the client pays you in full (this should protect your designs and copyright and encourage prompt payment);
- payment terms and when payment is due (this is usually 'by return'; you can even include a statement that interest will be charged in the event of late payment under the Late Payment of Commercial Debts Act 1998);
- a statement that you are VAT registered, if relevant;
- the date of annual review of your hourly or daily rates, if a contract is long term;
- a statement that the client will pay you in full for all of the work produced to date in the event of the client cancelling, changing their mind or not being happy with the project;
- a statement that the contract is not transferable.

The client must also guarantee that they own any branding or trademarks they provide for you to use or that they have full permission to use them from the owner of the copyright.

> *Once you have your carefully drafted set of terms and conditions, be sure not to waste the time and effort that you (and your solicitor) have spent on them by not using them. Be sure to get a signed copy or, if that is not possible, make sure you've sent your terms and conditions to the other party at all opportunities. Attach them to your emails, send them by registered post. Just make sure you get them across to the other side. If there's one thing worse than not having your own terms and conditions, it's wasting money on a set and then not using them.*
>
> Tim O'Callaghan, Solicitor, Arnold Fooks Chadwick LLP

3 Intellectual property rights, copyright and design rights

As an employee, the copyright of designs you create usually belongs to the company employing you. As a freelance designer, you own copyright in the designs you create for your client; they are your 'intellectual property' but the design right is theirs. Design right does not cover two-dimensional design. To protect your copyright, you must include a 'retention of title' clause in your contract, as an agreement to transfer your copyright once you have been paid in full. Failure to include this clause means that once a design from your illustration has been made into an actual garment, it may not be protected by UK copyright law.

Unregistered design rights require you to be able to prove that you have actual ownership of your design. An economical way to protect your rights is to send a copy of your design to yourself using a secure postal method that needs a signature on receipt. You must keep the envelope sealed with the date clearly visible on the outside, to prove the date you created your design.

As design rights only protect against the copying of individual designs, it is debatable whether it is worth registering them as it does not protect against any garment created independently that turns out to be the same by chance. Design rights and copyrights are covered for a specified number of years.

Add your own copyright to each of your designs, to declare your ownership and remind a client that you are aware of the laws that protect your design. A simple statement such as the following protects your rights:

This design is protected by copyright © Designed by ....
Date: ....

Note: Any computer files sent to the client must be in a fixed format (e.g. PDF or JPG) for security, to prevent alterations and to preserve your intellectual property rights. If a client asks for your original artwork in electronic form (e.g. your Adobe Illustrator document) as well as the PDF or JPG file of any work you do for them, I would encourage you to advise them that your original artwork is your intellectual property. It is up to you to agree at an early stage with your client whether you are selling your designs outright or whether you sell your client a license – the right to reproduce your designs for one or more specific purposes. Selling a right to reproduce is less common than selling a design in the UK fashion industry.

One client asked me for my Adobe Illustrator files in order to re-colour them themselves and save money on additional design fees. I pointed out that my designs are only available in PDF or JPG format, as they are my intellectual property. I explained they were buying the designs, not my original artwork files. They would own the copyright once they had paid me, as agreed by my contract. I suggested that they should pay me to re-colour the designs.

It can help to attend a seminar on the subject of intellectual property rights, design right and copyright law. Try UKFT (UK Fashion and Textile Association) or similar organisations for information.

4 Keeping yourself safe from prosecution for breach of copyright

Be aware of the rights of others to avoid prosecution. For example, should you use photographs that have been taken of garments you have designed yourself, you could be in danger of infringing the copyright of the photographer, the model and the company that paid you to design the garments. These people have rights over their work. Never use photographs without the copyright owner's permission.

Never use magazine images on any mood or trend boards that are presented to, shown to, left with or sent to a client. They could be reproduced in an inappropriate way leaving you open to prosecution. Use them only for your own research. The photographer usually owns the copyright of the actual photographic image and laws in the UK, the EU and most other countries protect that right. If you want to use it, you may need not just the photographer's permission, but also that of the models in the photograph, the model agencies and the publisher of the book, magazine or other publication in which you first found the image. Even photographs in the public domain that can be used without a license to reproduce or payment need to be checked thoroughly for copyright before even being considered for use – it is much safer and easier to use only your own images.

Designers should be aware that if they use photographic images from magazines and use them on mood boards that they could be found liable for breaching the copyright of the photographer. If you do not get permission from the photographer it is possible the photographer will sue you. If the designer has done the work on behalf of a client and the client uses the mood boards for their own advertising – the photographer could sue the client, and then the client counter sue the designer. Being sued could cost thousands of pounds or Euros.

To be sure, you should use only your own sketches and imagery on mood boards. Once these images are left with a client you no longer have any control over how they are used and they could be used in an inappropriate way.

- Never show confidential work to those not involved in it.
- Never use or copy trademarks, logos or other types of copyright-protected images on a client's work unless you have proof that they have the legal right to use them.
- Never copy a garment even if a client asks you: it would leave you liable for prosecution.
- Avoid anything you consider to be an infringement of copyright or intellectual property rights.
- Protect yourself; you could be the one who ends up in court, not just your client. It is simply not worth the risk.

5 Confidentiality

It is important that your client can rely on your confidentiality. Until products have reached the market, do not disclose designs to any other party even though it can be tempting to show a project with up-to-the-minute designs that you are working on. Inform potential clients that you are only able to show older work due to confidentiality.

Confidentiality of logos, branding and licensed products

Logos, branding, licensed products or other types of copyright information are usually sent to designers on discs or via email. They must be kept safe and never disclosed. You may be requested, and it would be wise, to destroy this type of information on completion of a project.

Keep your computer safe at all times and ensure you have a secure password to protect your work in the event of loss or theft. Keep backup discs safe for the same reasons.

I have been burgled and my laptop was stolen with all my work and personal information on it. I have been very careful ever since. I hide it when I go out and never leave it in the car (I had my car stolen once too). It would have been even worse if I had not backed up my work! Consider installing software that locates your computer in case of theft.

Ethics of working for competitors

A designer in full-time employment would normally work exclusively for one company. When working freelance, a designer is very likely to work for several companies at the same time. As designers tend to have specific areas of expertise, direct brand competition can be a problem. A client would be unhappy to find you also working for their competitors; however working on a different area is unlikely to be seen as direct competition. The wisest option is to be honest; your clients then know where they stand.

I was interviewed for freelance work only to discover that the brand was a direct competitor of an existing client. I was offered some work but in a completely different product area.

6 Keeping up to date with UK and EU law

Your client has a duty to adhere to UK and EU laws, which relate to the garments that they manufacture. As a designer, your responsibilities are normally for the design and development or manufacturing of garments but you should make yourself aware of laws and restrictions that apply to garment manufacture, distribution and retailing. This includes, for example, garment labelling requirements, restrictions on toxic substances in manufacture, laws on drawstrings on children's clothing, etc. Laws are often very different in countries outside the EU and you may need to seek further advice on this.

For UK and EU laws, UK government websites may help with basic information on legislation. One of the easiest ways to keep up to date is to join a trade organisation, such as UKFT. Often included in their regular emails to members is news on changes to existing legislation or new legislation worldwide as it affects our industry. A variety of different issues in this field are covered, such as employment laws, the minimum wage, pensions, equality in the workplace, safety, garment labelling and other important areas. Members can contact them for advice on specific subjects or for recommendations of other sources of guidance.

I was able to alert a client I was working with about changes in garment labelling legislation after reading my monthly email from UKFT.

7 How to find an expert on law in the fashion industry

There are different experts for specific areas, for example, there are contract lawyers familiar with and working within the fashion industry. For patent and trademark legislation and information contact a patent and trademark law practice.

Choose an expert in the specific area for which you require advice or assistance. A professional organisation may be able to recommend a suitable one; otherwise recommendation by colleagues or industry publications could help.

CHAPTER 7

Getting Paid

1 Chasing outstanding invoices

It would be good to be able to say that late or non-payment of invoices is very rare but that does not seem to be the case. Take steps to prevent late or non-payment by following up any delivery of your work to confirm the client has received it and then send your invoice promptly to encourage early settlement. Keep on top of all payments due and keep chasing late ones. A payment that is pursued is likely to be paid earlier than one that is not. Do not be fobbed off by a client if their payment is late; you have honoured your side of the contract and expect them to do likewise. If payments from a client are continually late, you may want to reconsider working for them and find a new client who values you and treats you fairly.

When chasing any payment keep accurate written records of all contact made with your client. Send statements and a copy of the invoice by email or post and check they have been received. Telephone your client's landline number, mobile number or even text at different times asking when you will be paid. Be firm and polite reminding them that your payment is late. You could offer to collect it if feasible. If you are told 'the cheque is in the post', ask for its number. When a company has payment dates, call and remind them that your payment is overdue.

If you have an ongoing agreement with a company, the same applies. You have agreed to a deadline for you to invoice them and another for them to pay you by. They should pay by an agreed method, such as direct payment into your bank account.

If you are worried about a client's ability to pay before you start working with them, ask for trade references, which you should then check. Confirm their trading name and address, if they pay on time and how long the referees have dealt with them. Check their credit ratings by contacting a credit reference agency or get a bank reference.

If you receive a cheque that bounces or is incorrectly written, call the client and ask for this to be rectified immediately. Keep a bounced cheque for evidence in the event of a court case.

2 What to do when a client fails to pay

When payments are late, depending on the payment history of the client, it could indicate underlying problems. Some clients always try to pay late; others who have paid promptly in the past may be encountering financial problems. Mistakes can be made but alarm bells ring if a second payment is late from a client who pays on time. My usual practice is to stop work until the payment is settled. It can be difficult to stop work until payment is settled if you feel loyalty towards the client, but you need to look after yourself.

The Late Payment of Commercial Debts Act 1998 supplemented by the Late Payment of Commercial Debts Regulations 2002 can protect against late payment.

Information can be found about these laws on the Internet. You may be able to charge for debt recovery costs on overdue invoices. The court website for making legal claims online is www.moneyclaim.gov.uk.

When a client fails to pay after numerous reminders, you need to consider court action. Ensure that you have fulfilled all your obligations within the agreed contract. The client may claim that they are unhappy with your work or may have another issue. If you feel confident that you have completed all that was agreed send them a letter by recorded delivery informing them that if they fail to settle within seven working days you will file a claim at the small claims court. This should encourage immediate settlement.

It is quite straightforward to write the letter yourself or you could pay a solicitor to write it for you. You could consider paying a debt recovery company to try and recover the debt or go ahead and file your claim.

3 The small claims court

It is possible to take a company to the small claims court if they have defaulted in paying your invoices, win the case, receive interest on the money owed and have the court fees reimbursed. Preparing the case for court takes up a lot of time and causes a lot of stress and anguish. It is time better spent working for clients who you know pay well or generating new leads. Using a signed contract and implementing it gives peace of mind.

Anonymous designer

The small claims court is your last resort if all other methods to make your client pay have failed. Court action may seem intimidating and complicated but is quite straightforward so do not be put off. If you have completed the work as agreed you deserve to be paid.

Check that the sum in question is within the small claims court limit; if it is higher you may need to seek legal advice. The small claims court deals with disputes over smaller amounts of money in the county court. It is less expensive and less complicated than larger claims and can avoid hiring legal help. Your contract is written proof of your agreement. A verbal agreement is still a contractual intention, though less easy to prove. When submitting your claim, you are required to pay a fee, the amount of which depends on the sum in dispute. You can choose a court near to you and track your claim online. For information about the small claims court and to make a claim, contact www.hmcourts-service.gov.uk.

Consider that your client may not be able to pay so you may not receive the money owed, even if you win, and you may not be awarded costs to cover the expenses incurred. You could check if your client is able to pay before you make your final decision to proceed. They may be in financial difficulties, have no assets, a history of bad debt, other unpaid county court judgements against them or be about to go bankrupt. As a precaution, obtain their bank account details (bank name, account number and sort code) and find out where their assets are and if they own any property.

Out-of-court settlements

When your client is served a 'claim pack' from the court, they may settle immediately. They will be required to reimburse the court fee you have paid as well as the original debt. When you are satisfied that the funds have cleared, you can advise Money Claim Online that the claim has been settled in full.

> *I was forced to file a claim when a client simply refused to pay their last invoice. They were always late with payments: two out of five invoices had been three weeks late. I telephoned, sent a copy invoice, a statement and letters, but they did not answer. I sent one final letter asking for settlement within seven working days or I would issue a court claim. They paid the invoice, but not the court fee, when they heard from the court. I finally visited their premises, with my partner for support, to collect the fee. I hope I never have to do all that again. It was very worrying. I am a member of the UKFT register, which was my lifeline. The staff were very supportive, guiding and encouraging me throughout.*
>
> Anonymous

What if it goes further?

The client (defendant) may decide not to immediately settle with you but to defend your claim. If that happens, the court provides you with a copy of the defendant's defence and then issues some directions for other steps in the litigation, such as disclosure of documents. You then have to disclose to the other side all relevant documents and emails in the matter and exchange witness statements, where you put in writing your version of events. You then receive details of a hearing date.

Another possibility is that the defendant ignores your claim, in which case you may request that judgement is entered against the defendant by default. You may do this 28 days after serving the claim form and you simply need to fill in a slip of paper and return it to the court. You then receive judgement against the defendant together with your court fees and possibly interest.

Once you have a judgement against the defendant, a county court judgement is registered against them. That, of course, does not automatically mean that you get paid. You need to consider how to enforce the judgement and there is a number of options open to you depending on the defendant's situation. You may, for example, apply for a winding-up order if the defendant is a company, for bankruptcy if the defendant is an individual or to send bailiffs in to take some of their goods up to the value of your claim. It is always best to consider your options at this stage with a solicitor, if you have not already done so, but the defendant's situation should always be considered before taking legal action against them. It would be a waste of time and money to sue a defendant who is already, or is about to be, bankrupt or insolvent.

CHAPTER 8

Planning Your Time

1 The working day

Working from premises is usually easier for self-discipline. You are more likely to work normal office hours than people working from home, which if you are not careful can be very unsocial and chaotic! But beware of late starts, long lunches and finishing early too many times. In both situations, you need to manage your time efficiently to have any hope of getting your work completed. Ensure saved travelling time is put to good use.

> *Working from home means you need to be very self-disciplined with the hours you work. It's so easy to have a bit of a lie-in or an extra pot of tea before you drag yourself to your desk, thinking you will catch up the time later in the day. Believe me, it's not that easy. I get more work done and feel much better if I get up early, shower, dress and breakfast before I get to my desk, aiming for no later than 9 A.M. I have a proper tea break, a lunch break and then try to finish work around about 6 P.M. Reality can sometimes be a frantic bid to get as much done as possible after a problematic or disturbed start to the day!*

It is not good to still be wearing your dressing gown at lunchtime if working from home. It is better to be up and dressed early. Plan your working days and weeks, setting aside time each week for administration. Avoid personal calls, family distractions and other interruptions. It can be difficult to settle down to work at times but it is very important to discipline yourself or your life could end up in a muddled mess with the feeling that work is never ending or finished. Avoid working at weekends to allow yourself a reasonable break, though at times that may not be possible. Working from home can make it difficult to turn a blind eye to domestic chores; it is easy to put the washing machine on as you make your morning tea but the ironing really does not need to be done during work time or you will never make a living! Separating your work from domestic tasks will help you concentrate and perform more effectively.

To help yourself to work more efficiently, make a point of going out each lunchtime. It will make you to feel more alert after sitting in front of a computer all morning. Try a spot of lunchtime exercise to refresh yourself; it can also help with any feelings of isolation.

> *I love the flexibility that working from home gives me but I do make a point of going out each day. If not, I find that some days I feel rather stifled to not set foot outside my front door! A swim when the local pool is quiet is relaxing; it soothes my mind and even helps me to resolve issues with my work!*

Organising and managing your time efficiently, wherever your place of work, will ensure you have a good work–life balance.

2 Your freelance diary

A working diary in which to record all vital information is essential. A5 (210mm × 148mm) is a good choice and a reasonable size to carry with you. An academic-year diary may be easier if you teach part time. Some people may find a computer or mobile telephone diary easier.

Enter exactly how many hours you work on which dates for each client; including times and length of meetings and telephone calls (computer time sheets to record and calculate hours worked are also useful, see Section 6). Some calls can last a substantial amount of time and need to be charged for: they often avoid the necessity for face-to-face meetings, saving the client time and money. Include details of expenses incurred during projects so that you are able to cost and identify them for each client. Record time spent travelling and the mileage for calculating travel expenses in preparation for compiling invoices. Be meticulous – if you miss something out, you are likely to miss it off your invoice and lose out financially. Diaries may possibly be useful if disputes over the hours worked or expenses arise. Store old ones with your relevant annual accounts for future reference.

I record everything in my working diary; it enables me to calculate invoices quickly and easily. I can look back at the time I spent working for each client and keep track of any expenses too. It lives on my desk and I never take it out with me to avoid it getting lost. It is simply too valuable to take that chance.

Your working diary will tell the whole story of your work; it is imperative to keep it up to date and accurate.

3 Holidays and your year plan

There are times during the year when it is just not practical to take holidays. It is obviously wise to book holidays during your least busy spells but that can sometimes be difficult to fit in with your personal life. Inevitably there seems to be a busy spell or much needed work available when your holiday is due. The way in which you work affects how you fit in your holiday times. You could simply book your holiday time off in advance then stick to it. A bonus can be the flexibility to choose less expensive times of year for a break. I often take my holidays out of season; it tends to be less crowded and much cheaper. I have had bargains when taking last-minute holidays, when I was not too busy with work and just fancied a break.

If you have a difficult year with little work, holidays can be hard to finance. Over the years, you are likely to adjust and adapt by careful saving and budgeting, making it less of an issue, but in the beginning it can seem daunting.

I was very short of work one year and was interviewed by a potential client a few days before I was due to go on a pre-booked, five-day break. The day before I was due to leave, I had a call offering me the work. The problem was that I was expected to accompany the client to a trade show in Paris during the time I would be away. I said that I would like to accept the work but was unable to make the trip due to my holiday. The client offered the work to her second choice; who accepted. I was unsure I had made the correct decision, but I could not let down my daughter and the friend I was travelling with. I was also really looking forward to the break. A few weeks later, I had another call from the same client; the other designer had not worked out and I was offered the work. I happily accepted and the job lasted for the next six years.

It could be a problem if you are called for jury service. David Robertson of Scullerthorpe, who is self-employed, chose to miss out on his summer holiday due to this:

> I was selected for jury service, which was to take place in August. At first I was annoyed, as this would normally have been the period I would have taken my holidays. As luck had it, I had not booked a holiday as normal and, being the month that two of the main markets I work in (Greece and Portugal) close for their annual holidays, I decided it was best to accept. Everyone that I had spoken to advised me that very rarely do you get selected for a jury and after a few days you do not even have to attend court. In most cases, you are requested to phone in and check to establish if you have to attend the next day. However, I was not so lucky. I was selected twice to sit on a jury and ended up doing service for three weeks, instead of the normal two. While it was disruptive, I did manage to work early in the morning and in the evening, following up on emails and general correspondence. The most frustrating point was not being able to contact clients and follow up issues and matters during normal working hours.

It is advisable to have a year plan and specify all of your holidays including Christmas, Easter, bank holidays in advance. This will enable you to actually book and take holidays, inform your clients when you will be away in advance and plan your work accordingly. Some years I have found it difficult to take holidays because of my workload or lack of work. I seem to either have too much or too little.

4 Interruptions and distractions

Interruptions can eat into your work time and vary dramatically depending on your circumstances, especially if working from home. The need to be self-disciplined is very important. You may get a variety of interruptions during the day. Other people may expect you to be able to tackle various tasks while you are working, particularly from home, such as domestic chores, shopping, looking after the children or your neighbour's dog, or acting as a handy taxi service.

I have often had friends and family phone me for a chat just as I am getting along nicely with my work. It is amazing that when you work from home some people assume that it's not 'real' work. People would not phone you at an office for a long personal chat! I have even had friends calling round for a coffee and a chat. This can be extremely distracting and very inconvenient.

Invest in a telephone that displays the caller's identity and do not answer calls other than business-related ones or it can give the impression you do not mind personal calls during working hours. If you do answer a personal call, say you will call them back out of working hours. If you install a separate business telephone line, keep it specifically for business and do not give the number to friends and family. This may sound harsh but a friend found that her sister would call her during working hours on her business line for a chat if she did not answer her home telephone.

Personal and work-related emails can be another distraction, with the urge to open them the minute they arrive. If you were to respond to each by return, you would never get any work done. You could try switching off from the Internet at specific times to avoid this. Read and respond to emails at set times during the day, maybe once during the morning and once during the afternoon. Answer personal emails at the end of the day to limit distractions.

Cold callers ringing your doorbell or unexpected visitors can prove difficult; you could avoid answering the door unless you are expecting someone.

The expectations of family and friends can be the hardest to deal with. You can seem unreasonable if you refuse or are unable to participate in certain activities during the working week. You cannot just take a day off when you want; you do actually have to work. It can be assumed that you are able to drop everything and you may become the first port of call when something needs doing or someone wants help. Unless it is a real emergency, you need to nip it in the bud and point out that you are working. Would expectations be the same if you were in full-time employment working at an employer's premises? Explain that you have to work to earn a living and have deadlines to meet. The stress when demands are made of you can cause problems to you and those around you. If you get really desperate you could always go out and take your laptop with you. In all instances, you need to be firm but fair and honest. It does not make you a bad person to say 'no'.

During good weather, it can be tempting to make excuses such as the sudden 'need' to tackle the gardening, but doing this during your lunch break would be wiser and limit it just to lunchtime. Another appealing prospect may be coffee with a friend, often difficult to resist!

> ' When the weather is good, a glass of wine sitting in the late afternoon sunshine with a friend has been irresistible. I think I will catch up later but my good intentions seem to vanish after the first sip! I end up working long hours the next day to make up the time! '

5 How to stand your ground when unreasonable demands are made

It is important for designers to be aware of unreasonable demands that could be made of them. The young and keen should be particularly wary to avoid being taken advantage of and promised all sorts of wonderful opportunities that never materialise. Standing your ground can sometimes be difficult and intimidating, especially when the client refuses to take 'no' for an answer.

Work now – money later

A potential client may suggest that you do a project for them now for nothing, with a promise of a future percentage on sales, also referred to as a royalty or commission. Don't be tempted! You cannot know how much a percentage would be worth unless they give you an estimate of sales – will they do that? Will they give you regular updates on sales? Unless you have a detailed contract agreeing all these details you would have no way of knowing what you are likely to be earning. It's extremely complicated and it seldom works.

Laurian Davies of UKFT explains:

> For example, the client explains that they are a small, new or young company, just starting out – or perhaps that they are established, but have not spent money on design before. Either way, they will try to get work out of you with the promise of payment when the collection you have designed sells. That's great for them; they don't have to outlay money upfront. But it's extremely unlikely to work for you for several reasons:
>
> • The client may not make your great designs up correctly, so they don't sell.
> • The client may make them up but their sales force don't know how to sell them or don't have contacts in the right area of the market to make them sell.
> • The client may make them up and get them sold but their production is awful and there is very little income.
> • The client may make them up, sell them and not get paid by their buyers.
> • The client may make them up, sell them and then go bust.
> • The client may make them up, sell them and then refuse to pay you.

The suggestion that you do the work now and get paid when the goods sell is usually just a way to avoid paying you. Unless you are working with a very large and reputable company which has a standard royalty contract (which will be long and detailed and include references to sales forecasts, length of time of the agreement, sales territories, etc.) to show you when you first start the discussions, and unless you are willing to wait (usually a minimum of at least a year) until you see income from your work, avoid this type of 'business arrangement'.

Request to carry company goods

If you are ever asked to carry company goods through Customs in the UK or overseas by a client in order for them to avoid paying duty, just say 'no'. This is nothing more or less than smuggling; it is illegal; don't do it.

Never carry any goods, money or anything else for a client or anyone through Customs. It is illegal. Be very firm – you could very likely be stopped by Customs and prosecuted. It is a criminal offence to fail to declare commercial goods and could mean a fine or even imprisonment. Your safety and security is paramount.

Advance funds for expenses

Your contract or exchange of letters with your client should detail how expenses are to be paid but I have been given all sorts of excuses why the advance funds I requested have not been sent. On one occasion, I informed a client that unless the funds were put into my account immediately I would not be on the flight for a trip I was to take on their behalf the next day, then left it up to them. Shortly after I received a call to say the money had been put in my account.

If you are asked to pay for something you do not feel comfortable about or are not confident that you will be reimbursed for, say 'no'. Do not even consider paying out for it. Ask for funds to cover the cost in advance.

Working unreasonable or difficult hours

This situation can be problematic and could even make the difference in accepting or continuing work. It really depends on what is asked of you and if you are prepared to accept it, but you should outline the basics of what you are agreeing to do in the letter of confirmation or contract which you give the client.

Tiredness has been a problem for me when catching very early, long flights and arriving abroad in time to complete a full working day, due to the time difference. After being up and awake for over eight hours, feeling reasonably OK, then working eight hours I felt awful for the next two or three days. It was due to flight times and unavoidable delays but I must admit I began to dread the trips as they just wore me out. Though I did love the work.

Travelling abroad to trade shows can be a minefield, as clients' expectations of your ability to function competently over a 24-hour period can vary dramatically. Departure on the 'red eye' and return on the last flight, avoiding an overnight stop, may seem good value to some. In reality, the designer is likely to be trying desperately to concentrate after very little sleep and excessive working hours, not functioning properly and not giving their best! Make it clear you are not prepared to work excessive hours and will function and work better if you are not exhausted.

I have tried trips crammed into a 24-hour period to save the client money. I believe this is false economy. In the past, I have been so tired by the afternoon I am past caring what I look at. These days I refuse to travel in the early hours to visit a trade show. I even suggested a client employ a different designer, as I could no longer face another trip. I now stand my ground and say I am prepared to travel the evening before and stay in a hotel nearby so I am fresh for the next day. I believe it gives the client better value as I function much better this way.

Accommodation

The client should always book and pay for your flights and hotels after agreeing timings and itinerary with you in advance. Expect a room to yourself – it is not reasonable to be asked to share.

Ensure you have the correct paperwork to prove your hotel and all your flights have been booked and paid well in advance of your journey.

I have been asked to pay for the room on arrival at a foreign hotel and been expected to share a room with a female employer.

Unreasonable deadlines

Some clients may try to set impossible deadlines. Calculate and stick to your own estimate of how long a project is likely to take and leave a bit extra for 'going-wrong time'.

I have been pressed to accept impossible deadlines. Once, after declining some work with insufficient time allowed to complete it, I found that other designers had also refused the work for the same reasons.

Unreasonable requests

I was asked to travel abroad with a client I had spoken to on the telephone but never met. As my only means of contact with them was a mobile telephone number and a hotmail address, I declined (see Section 2.3).

6 Computer timesheets

Computerised timesheets look professional and can make your life easier, being able to calculate the hours and even minutes that you work. If filled in accurately, they can save you time and are a very good method of recording your working hours. Use one timesheet for each client per week, month or project, based on your invoicing intervals.

A 'clock in and out' system is a good choice, calculating in hours and minutes. Another option is to simply log the hours you work, calculating hours and quarter hours. The spreadsheet can calculate the cost for each entry and give a final total.

It is important to familiarise yourself with the charts. Download an example chart and experiment with it to see how it works. If you find it difficult to understand, read the Excel instruction manual or consider taking a course in Excel.

Using the Clock In–Out Timesheet

Download the Clock In–Out Timesheet template from the book's website and re-name it. The downloaded timesheet contains two worksheets (see Figure 8.1): EXAMPLE is an example chart for you to experiment with; CLOCK IN–OUT TIMESHEET is ready for you to use. Click on EXAMPLE or CLOCK IN–OUT TIMESHEET at the bottom left to view the worksheet.

	CLOCK IN–OUT TIMESHEET					
Client:	XYZ Designs Ltd					
Invoice no:	XYZ015					
Hourly rate:	£50.00					
Date	**Work description**		**Start**	**Stop**	**Time elapsed**	**Total**
21–Sep–12	Jacket 9911		8:50	13:15	4:25	£220.83
22–Sep–12	Jacket spec 9911		14:15	15:45	1:30	£75.00
			0:00	0:00	0:00	£0.00
			0:00	0:00	0:00	£0.00
			0:00	0:00	0:00	£0.00
			0:00	0:00	0:00	£0.00
			0:00	0:00	0:00	£0.00
			0:00	0:00	0:00	£0.00
			0:00	0:00	0:00	£0.00
			0:00	0:00	0:00	£0.00
			0:00	0:00	0:00	£0.00
			0:00	0:00	0:00	£0.00
			0:00	0:00	0:00	£0.00
			0:00	0:00	0:00	£0.00
			0:00	0:00	0:00	£0.00
			0:00	0:00	0:00	£0.00
			0:00	0:00	0:00	£0.00
			0:00	0:00	0:00	£0.00
			0:00	0:00	0:00	£0.00
			0:00	0:00	0:00	£0.00
			0:00	0:00	0:00	£0.00
			0:00	0:00	0:00	£0.00
			0:00	0:00	0:00	£0.00
			0:00	0:00	0:00	£0.00
			0:00	0:00	0:00	£0.00
			0:00	0:00	0:00	£0.00
			0:00	0:00	0:00	£0.00
			0:00	0:00	0:00	£0.00
			0:00	0:00	0:00	£0.00
			0:00	0:00	0:00	£0.00
			0:00	0:00	0:00	£0.00
			0:00	0:00	0:00	£0.00
				Total =	**5:55**	**£295.83**
					Total =	**£295.83**

Figure 8.1 Clock In–Out Timesheet template

To prepare your timesheet, enter the following information into the appropriate cells:

- the client's name;
- the invoice number;
- your hourly rate (the chart will not calculate unless this is entered).

To enter the hours you have worked and use your timesheet, enter the following information into the appropriate cells:

- the date the work was undertaken;
- description of the work undertaken;
- the time you start working (in the format hh:mm);
- the time you stop working (in the format hh:mm).

The downloaded timesheet calculates your hours and minutes in the Time elapsed cell and multiplies it by your hourly rate to give the monetary Total column. The bottom row of the chart (row 37) gives the overall totals for this sheet.

To add rows to the timesheet, select the Insert option from the menu and click Rows. You need to add the formulas to any new rows, so it may be simpler to copy and paste an empty row that contains the formulas. Then double-check all formulas in the worksheet. Cells F37 and F38 should show exactly the same total. If they do not, re-check your chart formulas using Figure 8.2 as a guide. When you click on a cell, its formula shows in the formula bar. Make corrections in the formula bar not in the cell.

Remember: Double-check your charts to ensure they are calculating correctly each time you use them using Figure 8.2 as a guide.

Using the Hours Log Timesheet

Download the Hours Log Timesheet template from the book's website and re-name it. The downloaded timesheet contains two worksheets (see Figure 8.3): EXAMPLE is an example chart for you to experiment with; TIMESHEET (hours) is ready for you to use. Click on EXAMPLE or TIMESHEET (hours) at the bottom left to view the worksheet.

To prepare your timesheet, enter the following information into the appropriate cells:

- the client's name;
- the invoice number;
- your hourly rate (the chart will not calculate unless this is entered).

To enter the hours worked and use your timesheet, enter the following information into the appropriate cells:

- the date the work was undertaken;
- description of the work undertaken;
- the amount of time you work as hours (include part hours in 15 minute slots as a decimal number – 15 minutes is 0.25; 30 minutes is 0.5; and 45 minutes is 0.75).

CLOCK IN-OUT TIMESHEET					
Client:					
Invoice no:					
Hourly rate:					
Date	Work description	Start	Stop	Time elapsed	Total
				=IF(D6=0,0,IF(D6>C6,D6-C6,1+D6-C6))	=E6*B$4*24
				=IF(D7=0,0,IF(D7>C7,D7-C7,1+D7-C7))	=E7*B$4*24
				=IF(D8=0,0,IF(D8>C8,D8-C8,1+D8-C8))	=E8*B$4*24
				=IF(D9=0,0,IF(D9>C9,D9-C9,1+D9-C9))	=E9*B$4*24
				=IF(D10=0,0,IF(D10>C10,D10-C10,1+D10-C10))	=E10*B$4*24
				=IF(D11=0,0,IF(D11>C11,D11-C11,1+D11-C11))	=E11*B$4*24
				=IF(D12=0,0,IF(D12>C12,D12-C12,1+D12-C12))	=E12*B$4*24
				=IF(D13=0,0,IF(D13>C13,D13-C13,1+D13-C13))	=E13*B$4*24
				=IF(D14=0,0,IF(D14>C14,D14-C14,1+D14-C14))	=E14*B$4*24
				=IF(D15=0,0,IF(D15>C15,D15-C15,1+D15-C15))	=E15*B$4*24
				=IF(D16=0,0,IF(D16>C16,D16-C16,1+D16-C16))	=E16*B$4*24
				=IF(D17=0,0,IF(D17>C17,D17-C17,1+D17-C17))	=E17*B$4*24
				=IF(D18=0,0,IF(D18>C18,D18-C18,1+D18-C18))	=E18*B$4*24
				=IF(D19=0,0,IF(D19>C19,D19-C19,1+D19-C19))	=E19*B$4*24
				=IF(D20=0,0,IF(D20>C20,D20-C20,1+D20-C20))	=E20*B$4*24
				=IF(D21=0,0,IF(D21>C21,D21-C21,1+D21-C21))	=E21*B$4*24
				=IF(D22=0,0,IF(D22>C22,D22-C22,1+D22-C22))	=E22*B$4*24
				=IF(D23=0,0,IF(D23>C23,D23-C23,1+D23-C23))	=E23*B$4*24
				=IF(D24=0,0,IF(D24>C24,D24-C24,1+D24-C24))	=E24*B$4*24
				=IF(D25=0,0,IF(D25>C25,D25-C25,1+D25-C25))	=E25*B$4*24
				=IF(D26=0,0,IF(D26>C26,D26-C26,1+D26-C26))	=E26*B$4*24
				=IF(D27=0,0,IF(D27>C27,D27-C27,1+D27-C27))	=E27*B$4*24
				=IF(D28=0,0,IF(D28>C28,D28-C28,1+D28-C28))	=E28*B$4*24
				=IF(D29=0,0,IF(D29>C29,D29-C29,1+D29-C29))	=E29*B$4*24
				=IF(D30=0,0,IF(D30>C30,D30-C30,1+D30-C30))	=E30*B$4*24
				=IF(D31=0,0,IF(D31>C31,D31-C31,1+D31-C31))	=E31*B$4*24
				=IF(D32=0,0,IF(D32>C32,D32-C32,1+D32-C32))	=E32*B$4*24
				=IF(D33=0,0,IF(D33>C33,D33-C33,1+D33-C33))	=E33*B$4*24
				=IF(D34=0,0,IF(D34>C34,D34-C34,1+D34-C34))	=E34*B$4*24
				=IF(D35=0,0,IF(D35>C35,D35-C35,1+D35-C35))	=E35*B$4*24
				=IF(D36=0,0,IF(D36>C36,D36-C36,1+D36-C36))	=E36*B$4*24
			Total =	=SUM(E6:E36)	=SUM(F6:F36)
				Total =	=E37*B$4*24

LEGEND:

format cells = general
format cells = date = 14-MAR-01
format cells = time = 13.30
format cells = currency = -£1,234.10

Figure 8.2 Clock In-Out Timesheet formulas

97

TIMESHEET (hours)				
Client:	XYZ Designs Ltd			
Invoice no:	XYZ015			
Hourly rate:	£50.00		Include 1/4 hrs as decimal	
Date	Work description		Hours worked	Total
21-Sep-12	Jacket 9911		4.25	£212.50
22-Sep-12	Jacket spec 9911		1.5	£75.00
24-Sep-12	Jacket spec 9911		0.25	£12.50
				£0.00
				£0.00
				£0.00
				£0.00
				£0.00
				£0.00
				£0.00
				£0.00
				£0.00
				£0.00
				£0.00
				£0.00
				£0.00
				£0.00
				£0.00
				£0.00
				£0.00
				£0.00
				£0.00
				£0.00
				£0.00
				£0.00
				£0.00
				£0.00
				£0.00
				£0.00
				£0.00
				£0.00
		Total =	6	£300.00
			Total =	£300.00

Figure 8.3   Hours Log Timesheet template

The downloaded timesheet multiplies your time by your hourly rate to give the monetary Total column. The bottom row of the chart (row 37) gives the overall totals for this sheet.

To add rows to the timesheet, select the Insert option from the menu and click Rows. You need to add the formulas to any new rows, so it may be simpler to copy and paste an empty row that contains the formulas. Then double-check all

TIMESHEET (hours)				
Client:				
Invoice no:				
Hourly rate:			Include 1/4 hrs as decimal	
Date	Work description		Hours worked	Total
				=C6*B$4
				=C7*B$4
				=C8*B$4
				=C9*B$4
				=C10*B$4
				=C11*B$4
				=C12*B$4
				=C13*B$4
				=C14*B$4
				=C15*B$4
				=C16*B$4
				=C17*B$4
				=C18*B$4
				=C19*B$4
				=C20*B$4
				=C21*B$4
				=C22*B$4
				=C23*B$4
				=C24*B$4
				=C25*B$4
				=C26*B$4
				=C27*B$4
				=C28*B$4
				=C29*B$4
				=C30*B$4
				=C31*B$4
				=C32*B$4
				=C33*B$4
				=C34*B$4
				=C35*B$4
				=C36*B$4
		Total =	=SUM(C6:C36)	=SUM(D6:D36)
			Total =	=C37*B$4

LEGEND:		
		formal cells = general
		formal cells = date
		formal cells = currency

Figure 8.4   Hours Log Timesheet formulas

formulas in the worksheet. Cells D37 and D38 should show exactly the same total. If they do not, re-check your chart formulas using Figure 8.4 as a guide. When you click on a cell, its formula shows in the formula bar. Make corrections in the formula bar not in the cell.

Remember: Double-check your charts to ensure they are calculating correctly each time you use them using Figure 8.4 as a guide.

7 Backing up

Regular backing up of all your work is vital. It is a task that can be underestimated or overlooked. It is so easy to let this slide when you are busy, but it does need to be undertaken regularly and methodically. Sensible practice is to back up at the end of each day. A USB data stick can be used as a temporary backup medium for a limited amount of data, but always use another method too, such as an external hard drive, an online backup service or discs stored away from your place of work, in a different building (in case of fire and theft). If your computer were to develop operating system problems, be infected by a virus, have hard disk failure or be stolen, your work would be lost.

I remember friends losing all of their work: they had never ever backed up. I always back up twice, using discs for long-term backup, to cover the possibility of a disc not working.

CHAPTER 9

Training and Education

1 Extra training

Extra training courses to increase your skills and knowledge, while not essential, can be very useful and are always an asset if you can afford it. Courses and funding specifically for the self-employed and small businesses may be available if you meet the required criteria. Investigate any funding that may be available locally and regionally through councils and local colleges etc. Familiarise yourself with your local setup as regions do things differently. Try contacting Skillset for any funding that may be available to freelancers.

I have attended some very interesting and useful training courses: a one-day course introducing Excel and a two-day introduction to Photoshop proved valuable and fortunately I met criteria for funding. A few years later, I attended a short course at my local university. After successfully completing the course and examination, I gained a university certificate in web technologies with points towards a degree. Again, I was fortunate to find funding. More recently I have found some half-day courses very helpful. As well as helping me in areas that I had difficulty with, I met some interesting people from different industries during the courses. The experiences have enhanced my skills, enabling me to run my business more effectively.

2 Seminars and training courses for the self-employed

Some professional organisations regularly run seminars and some also run short courses aimed at freelancers and small businesses, some may offer members a discount. These cover many different aspects of business, for example getting paid, intellectual property rights, terms and conditions, working as a freelancer and many more. Some run specialist courses for the fashion industry including computer software training in Photoshop, Illustrator and similar. There are also courses and seminars specifically for students.

At times it can be difficult or even impossible to fit in extra training while working when self-employed, but during quieter periods it can work rather well.

Universities and colleges that specialise in fashion run a variety of short, part-time and evening courses that may be of interest. Some interesting and useful courses may be available during periods when full-time university and college courses are on holiday. It is worth considering universities and colleges local to you as well as those that are well known.

Your own research may provide you with many more options, sometimes in unexpected locations.

My sister was fortunate enough to learn couture dressmaking from the wife of her husband's colleague while she was living on a military base abroad. She also learnt specialist knitting techniques from another wife who designed and made her own knitwear.

3 Part-time teaching

Part-time teaching can be interesting and rewarding, with the added bonus of some regular income during term time. Classes and courses can vary from a few hours to weeks during the full academic year, depending on the institution and course. It may be more practical to consider working occasionally as a visiting lecturer rather than as a permanent part-time tutor as this is less restricting of your time and other commitments. Before considering or accepting a position, check the dates and class times to ensure it will be practical, confirm the hourly rate paid and exactly what is involved.

Part-time teaching is paid hourly for actual teaching time only; some work, such as class planning, you will be expected to complete in your own time. If there are meetings you are expected to attend, you will need to find out if you are to be paid for your time, if they are essential to your employment, when they are likely to occur and if they are practical for you to attend. If you know you will need to travel abroad for your freelance work during term times you should discuss this with the university or college. If you do choose to go ahead with part-time teaching you could find that it actually enhances your work; the students enthusiasm for the subject can be very inspiring.

If you decide that you do not have sufficient time to teach but feel the need 'to give something back', you could consider becoming a member of a university or college panel of experts comprising specialists working within the fashion industry who give up-to-date advice on the skills required and qualifications necessary for future employment within the fashion industry. This helps to ensure the course content is relevant. These positions are usually voluntary – unpaid.

Teaching qualifications

There are legal regulations about the qualifications needed to teach in further education (www.legislation.gov.uk/uksi/2007/2264). Contact the Learning and Skills Improvement Service (LSIS) for more information.

While a teaching qualification is an asset it could prove to be too much of a commitment for some freelance designers due to the time and fees involved in studying.

The academic year and time management

If you do choose to teach part-time, plan your time well and use it efficiently. Add the dates and times of all your classes to your working diary – an academic diary would be useful. Work, such as class planning, needs to be done in your own time and some will need to be completed before you start teaching. This is sometimes time-consuming but may be less so in subsequent years providing you teach exactly the same class and subject. Teaching can eat into your time but the amount of time required varies during the academic year.

When you are teaching, it will obviously take longer to complete a project during term time unless you work during the evenings and weekends. Take this into account when calculating estimates. A project may fall partly during the college holiday times. It can be difficult at times balancing part-time teaching and freelancing but mostly it works out quite well. It is really not that different from juggling the needs of several clients.

If you have a prior arrangement with the university or college you work for, planned business trips should not be a problem. Short trips may not interfere with the class. Your regular trade show visits each season can be beneficial for your students; they usually want to hear all about them and what they are like. They may even visit the same show for a college or university trip.

I was offered a part-time teaching post with an arrangement to accommodate my business travel. The 'scheme of work' for the academic year incorporated my trips. For the classes I was away for, the students were given work to continue at home.

If you are required to suddenly drop everything for a foreign business trip, it could be more of a problem. It would be wise to discuss the possibility of this happening before you accept a teaching position. The most straightforward solution would be to arrange for another tutor to cover your classes. If it were to happen regularly, it could interfere too much with the students' coursework and assessments and the continuity of the class.

PART 2

Preparing Work for Production

CHAPTER 10

Design and Development

1 Research and trends

Research is vital for all design projects and keeping up to date makes your job easier.

Keep up with current trends, styles, colour forecasting and new fabric developments at all times, including periods when you are not working on a specific project or are between jobs and looking for work.

Get out and about. 'People watch' in a variety of locations to see what they are actually wearing; look for quirky and interesting details. Visit shops and museums. Regularly attend trend prediction seminars and fashion and fabric exhibitions.

Constantly research using magazines and the Internet. Watch films and shows for current influences. Record and make sketches of all the information that you collect. Compile mood and trend boards each season that include colours, fabrics and silhouettes.

> *I believe it is vital for designers not to shut themselves away. A designer's life is about viewing the world and getting inspiration from what they see.*
> Chris Walker, Managing Director of Inspired Business Solutions

If you are always interested and focused and take note of up-and-coming trends, you will be prepared for any work that may come your way. It can be difficult to motivate yourself when money is tight or you are searching for work but never let your interest and enthusiasm wane. Your knowledge and up-to-the-minute information on trends and style are part of what your clients are looking for. Keep them up to date with relevant new trends evolving during the time you work on the project. They need to feel reassured that you really know what you are talking about.

I like to visit trend seminars each season. I find the information invaluable and use it constantly throughout the season. A seminar gives me so much information in a few hours, keeping me up to date, enthusiastic and excited for the coming season. I could never afford to finance research to the extent that seminars provide. It is also good to meet other freelance designers and small businesses regularly.

The following list gives a summary of some sources for research:

- trend prediction seminars: EMTEX Designer Forum, Scottish Textiles Industry Association;
- the trend library at EMTEX Designer Forum with access to Internet trend site for members; the UKFT colour and trend library;
- trend magazines and specialist fashion magazines available from Mode Information;
- fabric shows;

- trade shows;
- shops;
- museums;
- exhibitions;
- libraries;
- films;
- theatre;
- antique and vintage shops or markets;
- junk markets.

You can give old magazines and fabric swatches to a fashion department at a local college or university.

2 Working to a design brief

The written contract between you and your client will confirm the exact work involved in a project and can act as the design brief. Contracts and design briefs need to be adhered to and interpreted accurately. A verbal brief should be confirmed in writing by the client or you; both parties need to be clear on the precise work involved. During the work, if any alterations, queries or issues arise, talk to the customer to confirm their exact requirements and resolve any issues. There may need to be minor alterations to the brief as the project progresses; these need to be confirmed by both parties and in writing. If major changes are requested, it is vital to confirm them in writing.

Listen closely and carefully to your client when discussing their design brief. You are designing what they want for their target customer, not what you want or what you think they should have. Read design briefs carefully and consider and interpret the brief accurately. Look at it from the client's point of view. Chris Walker, Managing Director of Inspired Business Solutions, gives this advice:

> When working with designers, I am always very specific about colours, themes and styles. Some people do not want this: they want a blank canvas. I can usually tell these types because their eyes focus on anything except me! It is really important to ask as many questions as possible for you to glean information that will help your design brief. I believe you should look at this like a jigsaw: your client has a piece but will not show you; you, through questions, have to determine the shape of that piece then mould your designs to fit the jigsaw.

Having knowledge and an understanding of your clients' products will help you understand where they are coming from and exactly what they expect of you. Some clients will have a good idea of what they want while others may look to you for advice and guidance. Make sure you are as well informed as you can be.

> *I quite like to be given ideas within themes and like to see outfits thought out properly and put together. This is something my freelance designer and I worked on together and I eventually managed to save time and money with this method.*
>
> Heather Benhrima, Kasbah

Research your client's products. For each individual project, make sure you know the type of garments that your client has sold in the past and who their target customer is. Find out where their garments are sold, if they export; where do they export to? Look at their older ranges and catalogues to see how their ranges have developed. Visit their stand at a trade show, if possible, their showroom and websites or shops that sell their range. Consider the styles, colours, fabrics and trimmings they have used, the sizes they offer and the brands they aspire to. Their market position, price points and quality are also important. Ask clients which garments they have found in the past 'work' for them and sell well and if any have failed and why.

3 Concept and design, style or shape

The initial concept is most likely to originate from your client, either by further development from their existing brand and range or in a completely new direction. On occasions, there may be a new company with a completely new concept and brand to be developed, which can be very exciting. Discuss ideas and timescale thoroughly with your client before moving forward to the design and development process to enable your interpretation to be accurate and successful. Some compromises may need to be made as ideas progress and as the development process of the original concept evolves.

Consider the body shape, size and age range of the target customer; compile a 'to fit' body measurements size chart (see Section 12.10) for the range early in the development process, especially if the work is to include the full technical package. This will give you a strong foundation during the development of the products making the selection of suitable designs and colour palettes more specific. Clients like the fact that I consider all aspects of their ranges, especially identifying accurately their target customer's body size and shape. Many smaller businesses have never had their own size or colour charts developed and find wise 'colour decisions' and a 'good fit' difficult.

When designing garments that have a specific purpose or function, such as sportswear or uniforms, considerations of design, style, shape, fabric and colour can be even more significant. The age range, comfort and necessary movements of the wearer will make some styles and fabrics totally unsuitable. For example, close-fitting garments would be inappropriate for most workers and unsuitable for many jobs. Consider that workers may need to lift, stretch or climb. A more comfortably fitting garment with perhaps a percentage of stretch could be suitable. Very tight-fitting garments, short hemlines and low necklines would be totally inappropriate for a corporate uniform. Certain design features may also be unsuitable, for example, back pockets on jodhpurs would make them uncomfortable to wear when riding. Talk to a few people who will wear the garments and who participate in a specific sport or job to enable you to gain an understanding of what they expect, need and want from their garments. Restrictions in style or colour can apply in some circumstances, for example, in sports such as tennis and golf; you may need to comply with corporate colours for business garments.

Understanding your clients' exact requirements and target customer fully will enable you to produce a more suitable and successful range. After discussing tennis wear with semi-pro tennis players, I discovered that their actual requirements were different to what I expected or imagined them to be.

4 The PANTONE® Colour System

The PANTONE® FASHION + HOME™ Colour System is a vital tool used for product development in apparel, home furnishings and interior design. It provides colour control and aids communication. The system is ideal for creating colour palettes and it standardises colour worldwide, enabling designers to select and specify colours to manufacturers with accuracy and ease. Trend magazines often suggest specific PANTONE colours for coming seasons.

The PANTONE colour specifier (which recently introduced 175 new colours) now consists of 2100 tear-off paper chips (TPX). The colours are arranged chromatically and in colour families for ease of use. Each colour chip has a colour name and a six-digit reference number followed by 'TPX'. An index to aid in locating specific numbers and colours is included in the system. There are other PANTONE products available with cotton swatches (TCX) that include double-folded fabric swatches measuring 10 × 10cm folded (10 × 20cm unfolded) in the same range of colours. Each swatch card shows the PANTONE colour name and number on four strips so you can cut the swatch and use it as a design or merchandising tool.

The PANTONE colour guide fan containing the complete palette of 2100 colours is designed for portability and is a very useful tool for meetings, sample shopping and so on. It fans out to make colour matching and selection easier (see Figure 10.1).

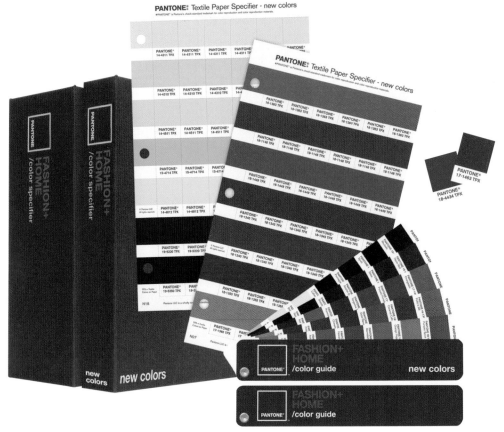

Figure 10.1 The PANTONE Colour System

The PANTONE digital colour library enables direct integration of the FASHION + HOME colour palette into compatible design software.

The PANTONE ColorMunki Design tool enables the calibration of your monitor and printer to match on-screen and printed colours to the PANTONE colour chips. You can also sample 'live' colour using the colour picker software (preloaded with more than 8000 PANTONE colours) to create your own colour palette and match to the closest PANTONE library colour. (Note: ColorMunki must be connected to a computer.)

The portable, lightweight PANTONE Capsure device allows you to 'capture' colours anywhere, add voice notes with a time and date stamp, match them to PANTONE colours and integrate them into compatible design software. It comes preloaded with more than 8000 PANTONE colours.

The PANTONE Textile Colour System® is available direct from www.pantone.com; contact PANTONE for distributors worldwide.

5 Colour palettes

During development of a commercial colour palette, you need to identify and take into account a number of considerations and issues.

You need to identify:

- your target customer or consumer:
  - age;
  - fashion attitude;
  - size and body shape;
- the purpose of the collection, e.g. fashion, leisure, sport (amateur, semi-professional or professional), corporate wear, maternity wear or childrenswear;
- the season, e.g. Spring/Summer 2014;
- the basic core product colours;
- traditional colours and restrictions, e.g. club rules or dress codes and specific colours for particular sports;
- comfort and suitability (e.g. white can be cooler to wear);
- highlight colours;
- whether warm or cool tones are required;
- colours that 'work together' as a range.

You also need to consider:

- displays in shops or catalogues;
- branding, which may affect the choice of colour palette;
- the frequency of washing (colour fastness issues could apply to certain colours);
- the type of fabric to be used: its performance and whether it is synthetic or natural (dye absorption may affect colour strengths);
- the skin tone of the target customers: some colours do not suit certain skin tones and would be unlikely to sell well in some countries;
- national or worldwide distribution and ethnicity of the target customer;
- the climate and season of the country in which garments are to be sold (e.g. brighter colours tend to sell well in holiday resorts).

Identifying your clients' (and their target customers') specific requirements will make the selection of suitable colours more straightforward.

I spend a considerable amount of time selecting a colour palette. I play around with individual colours making sure the combinations 'work' together. I leave them, then return to reconsider. I discuss them with the client to ensure they are satisfied with the final selection.

Colour can be powerful. When garments are displayed, a particular colour may stand out, attracting attention, yet basic core colours can sell in greater volume. A palette of only basic colours would be rather dull, but garments do need to be wearable and basics are needed. Bright and vibrant, or even subtle, colours are not for everyone but highlight or accent colours can make a plain or basic garment more noticeable and attractive and can be easier to wear.

A colour palette can make or break a range. Ensure it is suitable for the purpose for which it is intended, yet still in tune with current trends. Select colours and shades with care; utilise their power and capture attention by intelligent use of colour.

6 Branding

For an established brand, you may need to adhere to product branding; it is not always possible to change branding colours, which at times can be restricting. However with a completely new brand, branding needs to be designed and developed.

One large established brand I worked for supplied me with a large A4 file with all branding details, colours, sizes, fonts, restrictions, etc. as well as the artwork on computer disc.

Ensure your client has the legal right to use the branding they supply you with as copyright laws protect its use (see Section 6.4). If branding is already in existence, ask for it to be sent in the format you prefer. It is likely to be sent via the Internet or on computer disc and should be easy to apply to designs on computer. Once artwork is in your possession, keep it safe and never disclose it.

Establish your areas of expertise from the outset of any project. Some designers design and develop branding as well as designing garments, which can give a greater degree of control to the finished effect. If you do not offer this service make it clear from the start, as freelancers are sometimes expected to be able to do everything (often when the client wants to save money). It can be very difficult if you are pushed into work for which you are not trained or with which you do not feel comfortable. Some smaller companies may prefer to employ a designer who is very versatile and able to cover most areas.

One brand I worked for expected me to design prints and develop graphics as well as designing the garment range. I did have an interest in those areas but no training and I would wake up in the night worrying how I was to complete the project. A colleague suggested that I could employ a print designer and a graphic designer but there was no budget to cover that. I took a graphics course at a local college that helped enhance my skills and also used basic knowledge from my college days to enable me to complete the work successfully. I went on to complete a whole graphics course which I thoroughly enjoyed and it has helped with my work ever since.

7 Tickets and labels

There may already be established tickets and labels that link to branding and need to be used. They are less likely than branding to restrict colour choices for garments. Designers are more likely to be asked to design back neck or other garment labels than to design and develop swing tickets. Again, if you do not work in this area, it is important to make that clear to the client from the start.

8 Preparing roughs

Keep all of your research, sources of inspiration and ideas as evidence to support your designs and illustrate how they have developed. Some clients like to see roughs, a few prefer to select from them. Others like to choose from either presentation standard, hand drawn illustrations or computer-aided design illustrations (CADs). You need to establish at which stage the selection process will take place, as this affects the amount of time you spend working on finished illustrations.

A client who lived abroad preferred me to email small, simple, hand-drawn black and white illustrations with style codes to select from, rather than presentation standard hand drawn illustrations or CADs. It reduced the need for meetings, saved money and allowed her to see more ideas during the initial stages of development with an early opportunity for alterations. Later, I hand-sketched the selected designs in detail and I cut the first patterns from those designs.

9 Presenting your ideas to your client

Mood boards, trend boards and storyboards are important visual tools to communicate and demonstrate ideas. Always present your work clearly and professionally, even your rough sketches. No one wants to see tatty bits of paper stuffed into a folder or scruffy sketches. Your presentation and organisational skills speak volumes about your approach to your work.

Chris Walker, Managing Director of Inspired Business Solutions, gives a client's point of view:

> Designers can often communicate verbally but fail when the time comes to present their designs clearly. I think this is because they have researched thoroughly, worked on the design and so assume the viewer will like what they see. A good designer listens to the customer, researches and designs, and then explains how it works in clear simple language. Only following this process should storyboards be introduced. The storyboards should illustrate how the concept developed. If appropriate, a group of designs placed on one board enables the customer to see how each works together and complements other pieces.
>
> However, it is vital to ensure that design boards are not cluttered and over-full. Remember; keep it clear, clean and simple. The designer needs to understand that what the client believes he wants or needs is not necessarily what

the designer is about to display; the artwork needs to be sold. By presenting clear uncluttered storyboards, designers can easily discuss with the client how their designs match the brief. Coming from a non-design background, I find cluttered storyboards very difficult to examine and often wonder if they are cluttered because the designer is unsure of the presentation.

It is so important to communicate your ideas effectively to your client. Someone once said to me 'People don't see the world like you do, you can visualise and know exactly what a garment you have drawn will look like when its made and worn.'

It is very important to read Section 6.4. For copyright reasons, never use any magazine images on any mood boards, trend boards or storyboards that you present, show or send to a client. Only use your own sketches and imagery on mood boards.

CHAPTER 11

Presentation and Finished Designs

This chapter is aimed at fashion students and designers with basic knowledge and experience using Adobe Illustrator or similar software.

The detailed design and development process described in this chapter would be typical of a freelance designer working for a sportswear supplier or manufacturer (possibly offshore). The process may differ slightly in other areas of the industry and from company to company.

1 Using drawing software for presentation CADs

1 Presentation CADs

Most professional designers will be competent at illustrating their designs using computer software: Adobe Illustrator, CoralDraw or other similar software would be suitable. Fashion students will almost certainly have some experience and knowledge of CAD but will likely need to develop their skills in this area.

For designers who want to develop their skills further and those who have little or no experience, the most economic route is to work through training from books or CD tutorials and read the software manual from start to finish. This may sound very tedious but it really is a good way to learn. To become competent using software it is advisable to experiment and familiarise yourself with it. Your local library may well have software training books and CDs that could help you. Friends and colleagues who are competent using the software you have chosen may be able to give you advice, hints and tips. A short course could also help: they may be available at organisations such as Emtex Designer Forum or universities and colleges (see Section 3.2 and Sections 9.1 and 9.2).

Several friends and colleagues kindly spent time running through the basics with me when I first began using CAD. I found it quite difficult at first (I had never even used a computer before) but after a short time it began to get easier. I have purchased several books on the subject which has been a great source of information and they are very useful for reference. One in particular that I have found very helpful is *The Fashion Designer's Handbook for Adobe Illustrator 2nd Edition*. It is clear and easy to use.

2 Phases of a project

Projects can be separated into three basic phases for estimating price (see Section 4.1), planning time and working through.

- **Phase 1:** Research concept, design, style and shape, colour, branding, trends, suggested size range and garment type; garment designs (shown as roughs); a size chart showing the client's required size range. Roughs may be hand illustrated or prepared with CAD unless otherwise specified.

- **Phase 2:** Finished designs as presentation-standard CADs (A4 size in PDF) showing back and front views in full colour with up to three colourways, full garment detailing in black and white with fabric suggestions, and full details for any print, pattern, rib, labels, swing tickets, etc.
- **Phase 3:** Specification CADs (A4 size in PDF) in black and white, showing simple back and front views of each garment with an accompanying grade chart showing grade increments for each size, for a maximum of six sizes. Include sample request forms if required.

Some clients may require all three phases; others may require only some or part of them.

3 Phase 1: Preparing presentation roughs

There are several ways to present your roughs to your client; you may need to use different methods for different clients depending on their individual requirements and budgets. It can also depend on the type of garment to be designed and if communication is to be mostly by email or face-to-face meetings for the final selection of designs.

It is worth noting that not all clients want or need garments illustrated by CAD. Some may need only detailed hand drawn roughs, fabric and colour ideas and from there go directly to having first patterns and samples made.

Copyright

Add a copyright notice, your name and the date to each page of your roughs to protect your designs. It would be a good idea to print this onto every page before you start sketching (see Section 6.3). The wording is slightly different if there is more than one design per document (see Figure 11.2).

Style numbers

Remember to add a style number or code beside each individual rough design and also number each page or document so you and your client can refer to and identify your designs easily.

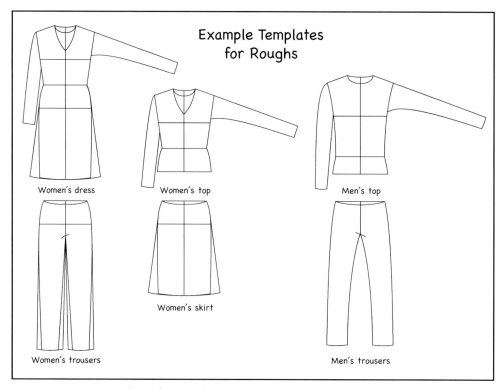

Figure 11.1 Templates for hand-drawn roughs

Hand-drawn roughs

You could present all, or a selection of, your initial hand-drawn designs, to your client (this may depend on how neat your initial sketches are). Some of the roughs could be included on your mood boards or storyboards.

If you prefer to use a template rather than sketch freehand make your own very basic garment templates like the examples shown in Figure 11.1. You can also download the template from the book's website.

These images can be enlarged if they are too small. Select a paper size to fit your scanner, i.e. A4 or A3. Using an artist's light box (to enable the templates to show through your paper clearly), place the template below your paper then draw your designs by hand, using the template as a guide. Depending on the template, paper size and type of garments involved; quite a few could fit onto one page.

CAD template roughs

A simple CAD garment template can be added to a basic pre-prepared CAD template (see Section 11.4) for a specific client (see Figure 11.2). Simply print out as many pages as you need and hand-sketch your ideas onto the garment template.

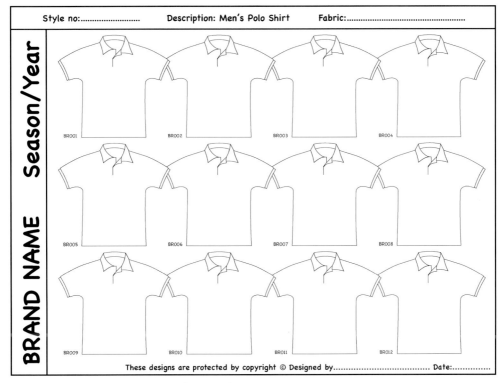

Figure 11.2   CAD template for roughs

Full-colour CAD roughs

Some clients may not want to see your very first hand-drawn rough ideas, preferring to see the initial designs as full-colour, presentation-standard CADs showing several different colourways, print or pattern ideas, branding design and other details (see Section 11.6).

It is not cost-effective or feasible to illustrate a large number of designs in this way and initial designs are likely to need to be amended at some stage as the range develops and progresses. In this instance, you need to select only the designs you consider most suitable from your roughs.

Colour ideas

You can add colour suggestions to roughs by hand, using artist's pens or similar media, or by computer. Some clients may be happy with black-and-white sketches at this stage.

Scan and email

When you have completed your rough designs, you can scan them into your computer and email them directly to your client for their selection if no meeting is required. If you choose to sketch in pencil you may need to draw over the pencil lines with black pen to ensure the designs scan clearly.

4 Preparing a CAD template for a client

Design and prepare a CAD presentation template for each client. The example shown in Figure 11.3 could have three layers when complete. The lower layer contains the basic template. Two other layers can be added in order on top of this basic layer to contain the garment details. Not all software packages will have layers.

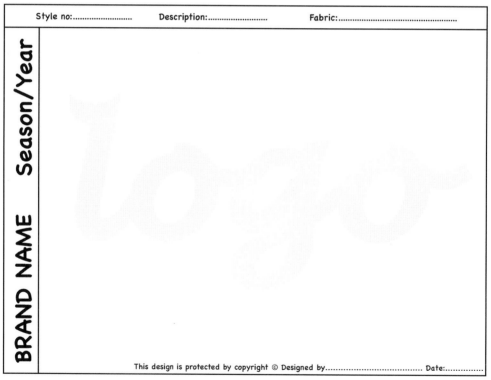

Figure 11.3   CAD template for a client

In the basic layer, include the brand name, season, year, style number or code, a description of the garment and fabric, your copyright, name and the date. You can also include a watermark image of the client's logo. The date will need to be updated each time any alteration is made to the document.

The second layer can contain the garment; the third can contain written garment details, trimmings, etc. Each layer can be locked or hidden and their order can be changed by selecting and dragging a layer into a new position. Extra layers can be added if needed.

5 Preparing a colour palette

In preparation for the final colour palette, design and develop a document in advance. Once the final colours have been selected and approved by the client, the palette can be completed (see Figure 11.4).

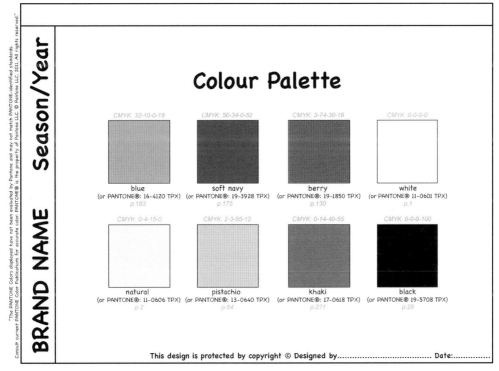

Figure 11.4   Colour palette template

It is useful to print an initial colour palette template with no colour in the swatch boxes. You can then experiment with colour swatches to develop your final palette. This template can also be useful for clients who are using 'off the peg' fabrics: the fabric cuttings can be attached to the colour-free swatch boxes.

Figure 11.4 shows the PANTONE® reference numbers and colour names (your own or the PANTONE names). Note that each colour swatch box needs to be a little bigger than the actual PANTONE chip to allow the printed colour to show on the paper when the colour chips are glued in place. The percentage mix of each colour (cyan, magenta, yellow and black – CMYK) shown in grey italic above the swatch and the PANTONE page number below can be timesaving and are intended only for the use of the designer. Alternatively, they can be jotted down in pencil on the designer's copy.

Match the on-screen and printed colours to PANTONE colour chips (see Section 10.4) by experimenting and adjusting the CMYK percentages of colour in the colour palette. Alternatively, you can invest in a PANTONE ColorMunki to calibrate your monitor and printer to match the on-screen and printed colours to the PANTONE colour chips (see Section 10.4).

A small version of the colour palette, including PANTONE reference numbers and colour names can be created and pasted outside of the printable area of the template document (see Figure 11.5). It can then be adapted to specify the colours for each individual design then added into the printable area (see Figures 11.6 and 11.7).

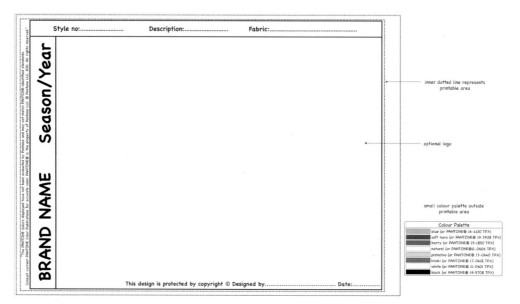

Figure 11.5   CAD template with colour palette

6 Phase 2: Preparing presentation-standard A4 CADs

When final designs have been selected from roughs, you can illustrate them using the computer. You will need to make a garment template, although it may be quicker to copy and paste a similar template, if you have one, and then make alterations to it. As you complete more and more freelance work, you will develop a collection of garment templates that you may be able to alter and adapt for future work.

Re-name the CAD client template (Figure 11.5) and copy and paste your garment template onto it. Using Figures 11.6 and 11.7 as a guide, develop your garment template in a separate document and save.

Make a duplicate of the appropriate garment template for each design. Give each individual garment design a style number (see Figures 11.6 and 11.7) and ensure that you use it to identify that garment at all times and to link all documents related to it. The style number could be the same as your rough, but most clients have their own method of garment identification coding. When you colour a design, add a small colour palette showing only the garment colours, with PANTONE references. Add any other necessary details, such as buttons, zip pulls, branding, print etc., plus any important notes.

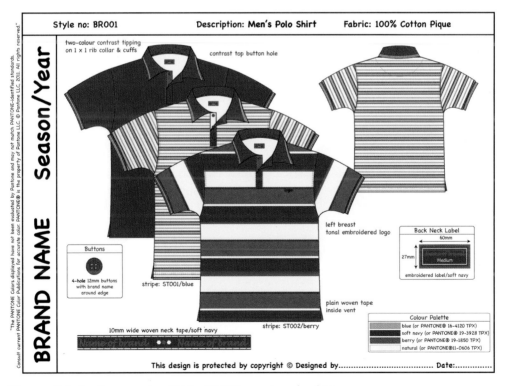

Figure 11.6   Presentation CAD: BR001 men's polo shirt

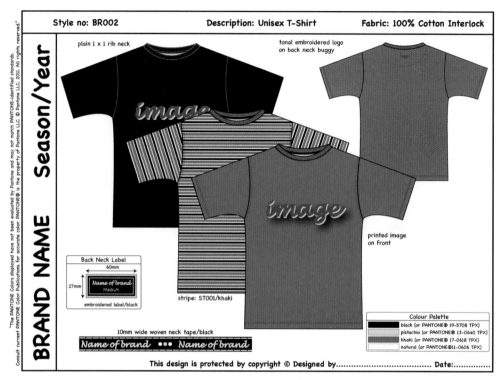

Figure 11.7   Presentation CAD: BR002 unisex T-shirt

CADs showing full garment details

Illustrations that show full garment details need to be predominantly black and white to allow all stitching and other details to show clearly (see Figures 11.8 and 11.9), however some items may need to be shown in colour and also specified in words. Arrows and written notes need to specify individual details clearly in order for the factory to know exactly how each garment is to look and how it needs to be made. Ensure all items and trimmings, such as buttons and labels, include colour with PANTONE references and size details. Sometimes it may be necessary to have one document per colourway for a design.

Branding details in full colour

Established branding may need to be illustrated in full colour and added to garment designs and presentation CADs. Branding could include the name of the brand or the logo as embroidery, a small label or print, a back neck label, a tape (often back neck), buttons, metal studs, a zip pull, etc.

Design and create new branding ideas in a separate document and then copy and paste your designs onto a re-named copy document of the CAD client template adding numbers or codes to identify each design (presented rather like the rough garment designs in Section 11.3). When the client has selected the designs, copy and paste them to a new presentation document to illustrate the final branding. Specify all details, such as fabric, embroidery, print, exact measurements and colours (include a small

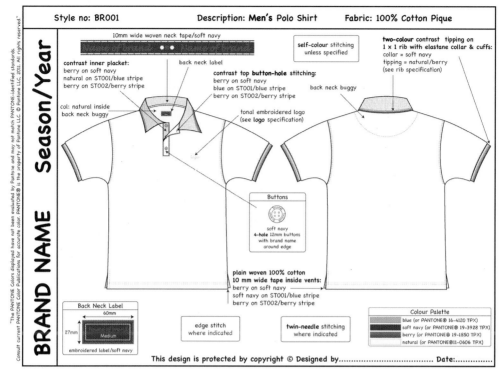

Figure 11.8 Full garment detail CAD: BR001 men's polo shirt

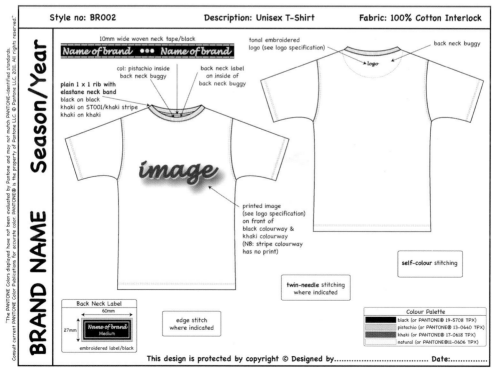

Figure 11.9 Full garment detail CAD: BR002 unisex T-shirt

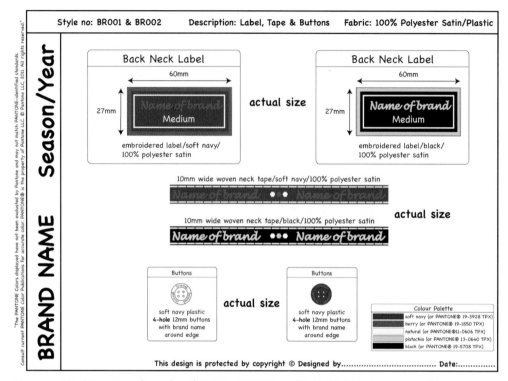

Figure 11.10 Branding detail CAD: BR001 and BR002 label, tape and buttons

colour palette with PANTONE references of the colours used) as shown in Figure 11.10. Items that are small, such as back neck labels, can be illustrated at actual size. They can then be printed and cut out to double-check that the size is suitable by trying them against sample garments.

Print and embroidery details in full colour

Print and embroidery details need to be presented on a saved and re-named version of the CAD client template. Any print or embroidery CAD needs to include all details, exact measurements and colour details including PANTONE references (see Figure 11.11). It must also specify if it is to be embroidery or a print with any other relevant details. Illustrate full, half or quarter scale if possible and always specify exact measurements.

Note: The embroidered logo for BR001 men's polo shirt is on the same document as the rib (Figure 11.16).

Pattern or stripe details in full colour

Present patterns or stripes in full, half or quarter scale on a saved and re-named version of the CAD client template. Give each pattern or stripe a code and identify each separate colour combination used (see Figure 11.12). Include a small colour palette with the PANTONE references. Check the size of the pattern or stripe against your

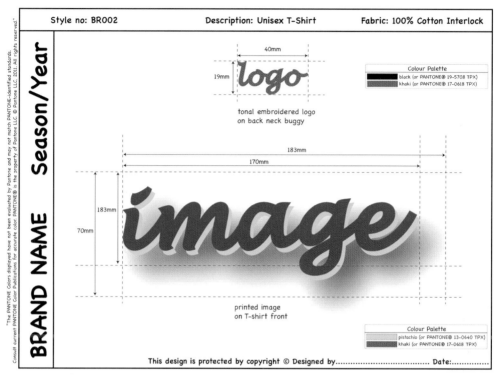

Figure 11.11   Print and embroidery detail CAD: BR002 unisex T-shirt

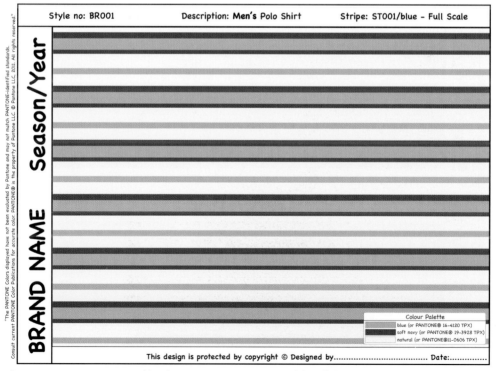

Figure 11.12   Stripe detail CAD: BR001-ST001/blue full scale

original CAD garment illustration and then create a full size printout to ensure the proportions are correct (see Figures 11.12, 11.13, 11.14 and 11.15).

Rib detail in full colour

Present the rib detail in full scale, if possible, on a saved and re-named version of the CAD client template. Give the exact size of any colour tipping (contrast colours on rib collars, cuffs or bottom bands) and remember to include and specify seam allowances in order for the rib to be knitted to the correct length (see Figure 11.16). Include fabric details and a small colour palette with the PANTONE references. Ensure proportions are correct.

Labels and swing tickets

Design and create label and swing ticket ideas in a separate document. Copy and paste your designs to a saved and renamed version of the CAD client template, adding numbers or codes to identify each design (presented rather like the rough garment designs in Section 11.3).

When the client has selected a design, copy and paste it into a new presentation document to illustrate the final label or swing ticket. Specify all details, such as print, font (name and size), card type, exact measurements and colours (include a small colour palette with the PANTONE references). Present final designs in full scale if possible (see Figure 11.17).

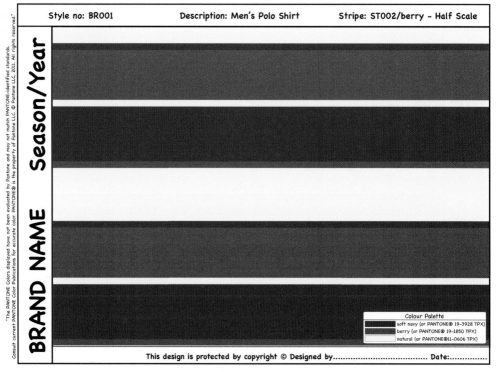

Figure 11.13   Stripe detail CAD: BR001-ST002/berry half scale

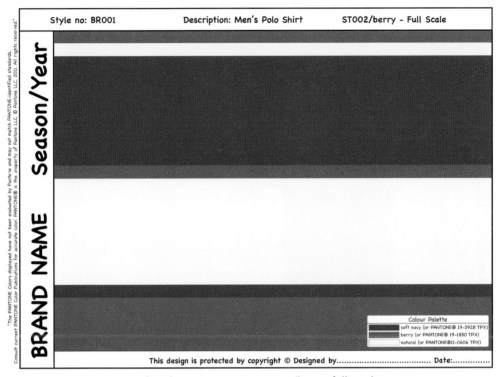

Figure 11.14 Stripe detail CAD: BR001-ST002/berry full scale

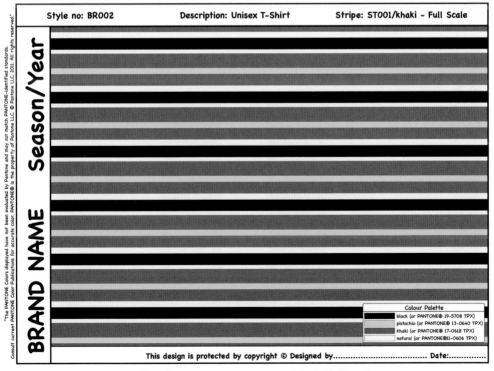

Figure 11.15 Stripe detail CAD: BR002-ST001/khaki full scale

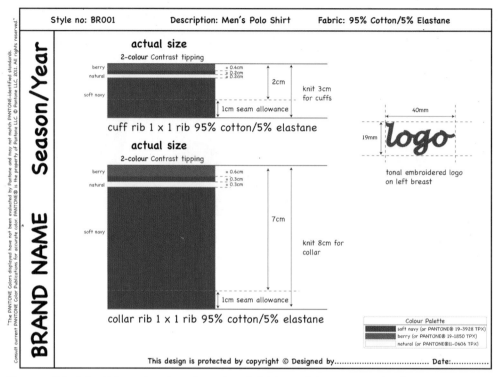

Figure 11.16 Rib and embroidery detail CAD: BR001 men's polo shirt

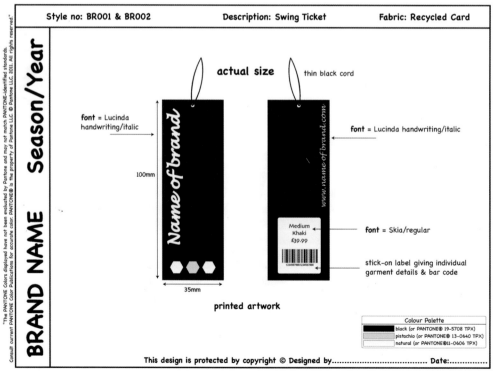

Figure 11.17 Swing ticket CAD: BR001 and BR002

7 Phase 3: Preparing detailed garment specifications

The detailed garment specification charts need to be very simple, basic, black and white garment illustrations and should include only essential stitch details, such as hems (see Figures 11.18 and 11.19). Add a dotted line to illustrate the higher neck point (HNP), from which some measurements start, and indicate it on the chart. Add arrows to show where measurements are taken from and to, marking letters close to them that match the letters specifying the same garment measurements on the accompanying Excel charts (Figures 11.20 and 11.21).

> *I never use the letters I, O, Q, P, V and U on specification diagrams (as a measure point) as they can get confused with other letters (U/V) or numbers (I/1). For front and back armhole grading, I grade straight, not curved.*
>
> Emma Wilson, Smartway Consulting

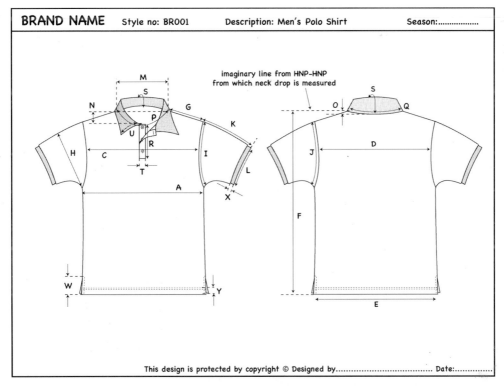

Figure 11.18   Detailed garment specification CAD: BR001 men's polo shirt

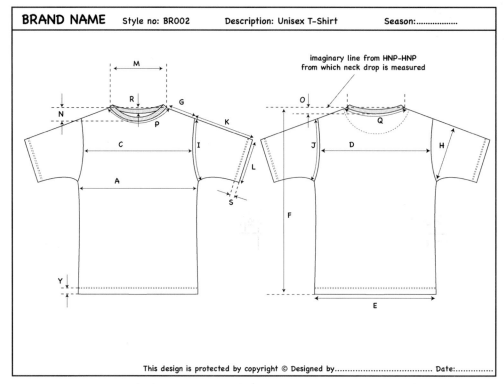

Figure 11.19 Detailed garment specification CAD: BR002 unisex T-shirt

Excel grade charts

Excel grade charts look professional and can make your life easier by calculating grade increments and measurements, as Figures 11.20 and 11.21 illustrate. They are also easy to use, alter and amend for individual garments. Chapter 12 discusses download-able template Excel size charts and gives instructions on how to use them. All Excel size grade charts need to be accompanied by a detailed black and white A4 CAD garment specification sheet (see Figures 11.18 and 11.19).

You may choose to complete the whole size chart before your first samples are made or include only the vital measurements, for example, chest width, back and sleeve length, plus any other measurements essential to the design in question. Other measurements can be left blank for you to calculate and complete after you have tested prototype samples for fit.

Sample garments need to be made and checked for fit. You should ensure that you see all sample garments. For comparison purposes, measurements taken from the samples can be noted on the size chart in the cell to the right of each measure-ment (the 'ins/cm' column). The size charts must be altered, if necessary, before bulk production (see Section 12.8). In Figures 11.20 and 11.21, the row labelled

Men's Polo Shirt (using 8-size chart with 1 grade)

Style no:	BR001		Season:								Date:		
Description:	Men's Polo Shirt		Fabric:	100% cotton pique							Grade:	Men's	
Brand:			Trim:										

		36	38	40	42	44	46	48	50	GRADE INC		TOL +/-	
To fit chest inches		36	38	40	42	44	46	48	50	ins	2	inches	
To fit chest cms		92	97	102	107	112	117	122	127	cms	5	cms	
UK size		XS	S	M	L	XL	XXL	XXXL	XXXXL				
A	Chest (2.5cm below a/hole, 1/2 flat)	52	54.5	57	59.5	62	64.5	67	69.5		2.5	1	cms
B	Waist (1/2 flat)	0	0	0	0	0	0	0	0		0		cms
C	Across front (14cm from HNP)	43	43	43	43	43	43	43	43			0.5	cms
D	Across back (14cm from HNP)	44	44	44	44	44	44	44	44			0.5	cms
E	Bottom width (1/2 flat)	52	54.5	57	59.5	62	64.5	67	69.5		2.5	1	cms
F	Back length (HNP-bottom)	69	70.5	72	73.5	75	76.5	78	79.5		1.5	1	cms
G	Shoulder length	16.7	17.1	17.5	17.9	18.3	18.7	19.1	19.5		0.4	0.5	cms
H	Bicep (1/2 flat)	21	22	23	24	25	26	27	28		1	0.5	cms
I	Armhole front (1/2 curved)	23	24	25	26	27	28	29	30		1	1	cms
J	Armhole back (1/2 curved)	23	24	25	26	27	28	29	30		1	1	cms
K	Sleeve length (overarm)	20.4	20.7	21	21.3	21.6	21.9	22.2	22.5		0.3	1	cms
L	Rib cuff width relaxed (1/2 flat)	15.3	15.3	15.3	15.3	15.3	15.3	15.3	15.3			0.5	cms
M	Neck width (HNP-HNP)	17.5	17.5	17.5	17.5	17.5	17.5	17.5	17.5			0.5	cms
N	Front neck drop (from imaginary line)	7.5	7.5	7.5	7.5	7.5	7.5	7.5	7.5			0.5	cms
O	Back neck drop (from imaginary line)	1.5	1.5	1.5	1.5	1.5	1.5	1.5	1.5			0.5	cms
P & Q	Neck circumference	39.6	40.8	42	43.2	44.4	45.6	46.8	48		1.2	0.5	cms
P	Front neck (inc fastened placket)	24	24	24	24	24	24	24	24			0.5	cms
Q	Back neck seam	18	18	18	18	18	18	18	18			0.5	cms
R	Front placket length	14.5	14.5	14.5	14.5	14.5	14.5	14.5	14.5		0	0.5	cms
S	Rib collar depth CBN	6.7	6.7	6.7	6.7	6.7	6.7	6.7	6.7		0	0.5	cms
T	Front placket width	3	3	3	3	3	3	3	3		0	0.5	cms
U	Rib collar points	6.5	6.5	6.5	6.5	6.5	6.5	6.5	6.5		0	0.5	cms
V	Collar stand depth	0	0	0	0	0	0	0	0		0		cms
W	Side vent depth	4.5	4.5	4.5	4.5	4.5	4.5	4.5	4.5		0	0.5	cms
X	Sleeve rib depth	1.7	1.7	1.7	1.7	1.7	1.7	1.7	1.7		0	0.5	cms
Y	Hem depth	2.5	2.5	2.5	2.5	2.5	2.5	2.5	2.5		0	0.5	cms
Z	Contrast stripe width	0	0	0	0	0	0	0	0		0		cms

garment measurements This design is protected by copyright © Designed by:................................ Date:.............

This chart is to be used as a guide only. Any similarity to any other chart is coincidental. The author and publisher do not accept any liability.

Figure 11.20 Excel grade chart: BR001 men's polo shirt

Unisex T-shirt for 6 sizes (using 8-size chart with 2 grades)

Style no:	BR002		Season:			Date:
Description:	Unisex T-Shirt				Grade:	Unisex adult
Brand:		Fabric:	100% cotton			
Trim:			1 x 1 rib 95% cotton/5% elastane			

		XXS	XS	S	M	GRADE INC (2 / 5)	L	XL	XXL	XXXL	GRADE INC (3 / 7.5)	TOL +/- ins	
To fit chest inches		32	34	36	38		41	44	47	50		inches	
To fit chest cms		81.5	86.5	91.5	96.5		104	111.5	119	126.5		cms	
A	Chest (2.5cm below a/hole, 1/2 flat)	47	49.5	52	54.5	2.5	58.25	62	65.75	69.5	3.75	1	cms
B	Waist (1/2 flat)	-4.5	-3	-1.5	0	1.5	0	0	0	0	0		cms
C	Across front (14cm from HNP)	42	42	42	42		42	42	42	42		0.5	cms
D	Across back (14cm from HNP)	42	42	42	42		42	42	42	42		0.5	cms
E	Bottom width (1/2 flat)	47	49.5	52	54.5	2.5	58.25	62	65.75	69.5	3.75	1	cms
F	Back length (HNP-bottom)	66.5	68	69.5	71	1.5	73	75	77	79	2	1	cms
G	Shoulder length	15.8	16.2	16.6	17	0.4	17.6	18.2	18.8	19.4	0.6	0.5	cms
H	Bicep (1/2 flat)	19	20	21	22	1	23.5	25	26.5	28	1.5	0.5	cms
I	Armhole front (1/2 curved)	21.5	22.5	23.5	24.5	1	26	27.5	29	30.5	1.5	1	cms
J	Armhole back (1/2 curved)	21.5	22.5	23.5	24.5	1	26	27.5	29	30.5	1.5	1	cms
K	Sleeve length (overarm)	20.1	20.4	20.7	21	0.3	21.5	22	22.5	23	0.5	1	cms
L	Sleeve width (1/2 flat)	18	18	18	18		18	18	18	18		0.5	cms
M	Neck width (HNP-HNP)	17	17	17	17		17	17	17	17		0.5	cms
N	Front neck drop (from imaginary line)	7.5	7.5	7.5	7.5		7.5	7.5	7.5	7.5		0.5	cms
O	Back neck drop (from imaginary line)	2	2	2	2		2	2	2	2		0.5	cms
P & Q	Neck circumference	40.4	41.6	42.8	44	1.2	45.8	47.6	49.4	51.2	1.8		cms
P	Front neck seam (below rib)	26	26	26	26		26	26	26	26		0.5	cms
Q	Back neck seam (below rib)	18	18	18	18		18	18	18	18		0.5	cms
R	Neck rib depth	2	2	2	2		2	2	2	2		0.5	cms
S	Sleeve hem depth	2	2	2	2	0	2	2	2	2	0	0.5	cms
T	Front placket width	-4.5	-3	-1.5	0	1.5	0	0	0	0	0		cms
U	Collar points	-4.5	-3	-1.5	0	1.5	0	0	0	0			cms
V	Collar stand depth	-4.5	-3	-1.5	0	1.5	0	0	0	0			cms
W	Side vent depth	-4.5	-3	-1.5	0	1.5	0	0	0	0			cms
X	Sleeve rib depth	-4.5	-3	-1.5	0	1.5	0	0	0	0			cms
Y	Hem depth	2	2	2	2	0	2	2	2	2	0	0.5	cms
Z		-4.5	-3	-1.5	0	1.5	0	0	0	0			cms

garment measurements

Figure 11.21 Excel grade chart: BR002 unisex T-shirt

'P & Q' gives the total neck circumference rather than stating the front and back neck measurements.

> " *I never add across-chest measurements, unless it is pertinent to the design.* "
>
> Emma Wilson, Smartway Consulting

It is important to be aware that there may be no direct communication between you and the pattern cutter, grader or manufacturer. You need to ensure that your charts are as accurate as possible.

Figure 11.20 illustrates a fully completed size chart ready for sampling for a men's polo shirt with eight sizes and one grade increment column. Figure 11.21 illustrates a size chart (also ready for sampling) for a unisex T-shirt size chart, showing only six of the eight sizes on the chart. Please note that the measurements and grade increments on these charts are the figures that I find work for me, others may use slightly different figures.

In Figure 11.21, the measurement columns at each end (the smallest and largest sizes) have had the text coloured white so that they are not visible thus showing only the required sizes. This chart also illustrates a unisex grade that has two increment columns, a one size grade (5cm/2" chest) in one increment column between the smaller sizes and then a one and a half size grade (7.5cm/3") in a second column of increments between the larger sizes (this method is also sometimes used for plus sizes).

Sample request forms

The sample request forms in Figures 11.22 and 11.23 compile and specify all items needed to make the garments in all colourways. They include brand, style code, colourways, date, type of grade (men's, women's, children's or unisex), size range (S, M, L or 10, 12, 14, etc.), a description of the garment, the quantity and size of samples requested and the date required. They also specify fabric details, with any manufacturer's reference codes (the manufacturer may need to be added), colours, description, width, weight and composition, lining, interfacing, quilting and all trimmings, such as buttons, zip, zip pull, tape, labels, logos, embroideries, prints, thread, etc. The fastening direction (men's or ladies'), the position of certain labels and the washing instructions are all included.

Figure 11.21 corresponds to the sample request form for the T-shirt (Figure 11.23), which states the sizes required for sampling: XS, S, M, L, XL, XXL. In this example, the largest (XXXL) and smallest (XXS) sizes are not required.

You can download a sample request form template from the book's website (see Figure 11.24). Save the document and re-name it.

SAMPLE REQUEST FORM					
Style	BR001	Colours	3 as below	Date	
Brand		Grade	Mens	Size Range	XS/S/M/L/XL/XXL/XXXL/XXXXL
Description	Short sleeved polo shirt	Quantity required	1 of each size	Date required	ASAP

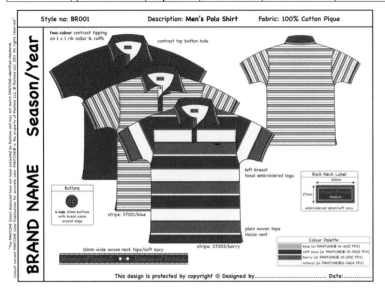

FABRIC/Company/Code	Description	Width	Weight	Composition	Colour
Fabric 1/Code:	Plain knit	152/5 cm	140 g	100% cotton pique	Soft navy
Fabric 2/Code:	Stripe knit ST001/blue	140/4 cm	140 g	100% cotton pique	Blue/soft navy/ natural
Fabric 3/Code:	Stripe knit ST002/berry	140/4 cm	140 g	100% cotton pique	Soft navy/berry/ natural
Fabric 4/Code:	Plain knit	152/5 cm	140 g	100% cotton pique	Natural
Fabric 5/Code:	Plain knit	152/5 cm	140 g	100% cotton pique	Berry
Interfacing/Code:	Soft				
Rib/Code:	Collar 1 x 1 knit rib			95% cotton/5% elastane	Soft navy/berry/ natural
Rib/Code:	Cuffs 1 x 1 knit rib			95% cotton/5% elastane	Soft navy/berry/ natural
TRIM/Company/Code	Description	Size		Quantity	Colour
Buttons/Code:	4 hole as spec	12mm		3 + 1 spare	Soft navy
Tape/Code:	Branded tape	10mm wide			Soft navy
Tape/Code:	Plain 100% cotton woven tape	10mm wide			Berry/soft navy
Logo/Code:	Embroidered logo	As spec		1	Tonal
Emb/Print/Code:					
Back neck Label	As spec	As spec		1	Soft navy
Thread/Code:	100% polyester				As main col
Fastening Direction	Mens left over right				
Label Position	Back neck				
Washing Instructions					
Care Label Position	Lower left side seam (inside)				

Figure 11.22 Sample request form: BR001 men's polo shirt

SAMPLE REQUEST FORM					
Style	BR002	Colours	3 as below	Date	
Brand		Grade	Unisex	Size Range	XS/S/M/L/XL/XXL
Description	Short sleeved T-shirt	Quantity required	1 of each size	Date required	ASAP

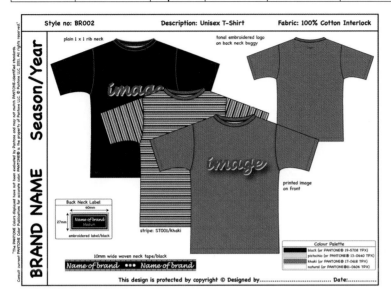

FABRIC/Company/Code	Description	Width	Weight	Composition	Colour
Fabric 1/Code:	Plain knit	152/5 cm	180 g	100% cotton interlock	Black
Fabric 2/Code:	Stripe knit ST003	152/5 cm	180 g	100% cotton interlock	Black/pistachio/ khaki/natural
Fabric 3/Code:	Plain knit	152/5 cm	180 g	100% cotton interlock	Khaki
Fabric 4/Code:	Plain knit	152/5 cm	180 g	100% cotton interlock	Pistachio
Fabric 5/Code:					
Interfacing/Code:					
Rib/Code:	Neck 1 x 1 knit rib			95% cotton/5% elastane	Black/khaki

TRIM/Company/Code	Description	Size	Quantity	Colour
Buttons/Code:				
Tape/Code:	Branded tape	10 mm wide		Black
Tape/Code:				
Logo/Code:	Embroidered logo	As spec	1	Tonal
Emb/Print/Code:	Print	As spec	1	As spec
Back neck Label	As spec	As spec	1	Black
Thread/Code:	100% polyester			As main col
Fastening Direction				
Label Position	Back neck			
Washing Instructions				
Care Label Position	Lower left side seam (inside)			

Figure 11.23 Sample request form: BR002 unisex T-shirt

SAMPLE REQUEST FORM					
Style		Colours		Date	
Brand		Grade		Size Range	
Description		Quantity required		Date required	

FABRIC/Company/Code	Description	Width	Weight	Composition	Colour
Fabric 1/Code:					
Fabric 2/Code:					
Fabric 3/Code:					
Fabric 4/Code:					
Fabric 5/Code:					
Interfacing/Code:					
Rib/Code:					
Rib/Code:					
TRIM/Company/Code	Description	Size		Quantity	Colour
Buttons/Code:					
Tape/Code:					
Tape/Code:					
Logo/Code:					
Emb/Print/Code:					
Back neck Label					
Thread/Code:					
Fastening Direction					
Label Position					
Washing Instructions					
Care Label Position					

Figure 11.24   Sample request form template

To use your chart, enter the following information into the appropriate cells:

- style code;
- number of colourways;
- date;
- brand;
- grade (men's, women's, children's or unisex);
- size range (e.g. S, M, L or 10, 12, 14);
- garment description;
- quantity and size of samples required;
- date samples required;
- all fabric details: fabric company, fabric details (e.g. plain knit, stripe knit ST001), plus any manufacturer's reference codes, width, weight, composition, description, (e.g. 100% cotton pique) and colours (e.g. soft navy, berry and natural);
- linings, interfacing, filler, quilting plus any other materials needed;
- trimmings and details;
- print and embroidery details;
- thread colours;
- fastening direction;
- label positions;
- washing instructions.

Insert a colour image of the design showing all colourways into the middle of the form (as in Figures 11.22 and 11.23). To insert the image, select the Insert menu and then select Picture, From File. You will need to reduce the size of the image in order for the form to fit onto A4.

Ensure the chart is filled in correctly.

Note: It is important to familiarise yourself with the charts and how they work. Download an example chart and experiment with it. If you find it difficult, read your Word instruction manual or consider taking a beginners' class.

8 Compiling the full technical package

A full technical package for one garment consists of most of the elements illustrated in this chapter. It comprises all the documents to be sent to the factory, giving the complete information necessary to make the garment. Individual garments are usually part of a range and the common information is usually given as a separate 'collection' package.

Collection information for BR001 men's polo shirt and BR002 unisex T-shirt consists of:

- the presentation roughs;
- a colour palette;

- the swing ticket design;
- branding details in full colour – back neck label, neck tape and buttons (all in the same document).

The full technical pack for the BR001 men's polo shirt consists of:

- a sample request form;
- presentation-standard A4 CADs in full colour;
- a detailed garment specification;
- stripe details in full colour;
- embroidery details in full colour (on the same document as the rib);
- the rib detail in full colour;
- a full garment detailing CAD;
- the Excel grade chart.

The full technical pack for the BR002 unisex T-shirt consists of:

- a sample request form;
- presentation-standard A4 CADs in full colour;
- a detailed garment specification;
- stripe details in full colour;
- print and embroidery details in full colour (on the same document);
- a full garment detailing CAD;
- the Excel grade chart.

9 References

Centner, M. and Vereker, F. (2011) *The Fashion Designer's Handbook for Adobe Illustrator*, 2nd edition. John Wiley & Sons, Ltd.

CHAPTER 12

Sizing

Note: This information is for general reference and guidance only; the author and publisher accept no liability for its contents.

1 Sizing issues

Sizing and fit are frequently a problem area. Consumers want garments that fit their bodies well, but achieving this can prove difficult. For volume manufacturing, this can create a wide range of problems. For example, within any one given garment size individual bodies can vary considerably. We need to take into account gender, body shape and build (athletic, slim or curvy), proportions, height, arm and leg lengths, thinness, obesity, ethnicity, ageing and pregnancy. 'Plus' sizing for adults and children is essential as more people become overweight. As people age, posture changes and weight and size tend to increase while height can reduce. In spite of all these difficulties, we need to ensure garments fit consistently.

One job I undertook involved designing a uniform for men and women aged from 16 to 65 and over. This is not easy when the client requests one set of garments to fit and suit all ages and sizes.

It is also important to consider that retailers and manufacturers can call a garment any size they choose: 1, 2, 3; S, M, L; 10, 12, 14, etc. The body shape and size that these garment sizes fit can vary considerably. This is discussed more fully in Sections 12.3 and 12.4.

In the course of my work and research, I have found that many people actually delude themselves as to their true size. It can prove very interesting to conduct your own small survey by taking the measurements of a few willing friends and asking what size clothes they buy, where they tend to buy from and why. You can then compare the results.

Children's sizing has its own set of issues. Their garments are generally sized by age or height guides intended to aid the consumer but, as children come in different shapes and sizes and do not conveniently grow at the same pace, this method of sizing can be deceptive. It can help the consumer by giving a 'to fit' body measurement, such as the chest or waist measurement.

Since the major sizing survey taken during the 1950s, the average body shape has changed, which illustrates the importance of revising sizing regularly. Three-dimensional body scanners now aid research; in seconds they can accurately measure a person, even including measurements of the left and right sides of the body. They are an effective and efficient means of gathering information. This can aid in identifying body shapes for target markets and help garment fit and size.

In reality, people's bodies are unlikely to correspond to convenient equal and specific grade increments between sizes, as recent sizing information indicates, or to just one generalised basic size chart for all men or all women. Therefore, different charts need to be compiled and used for different target customers. Each grade should be considered as individual increments, not necessarily averaged or linear as has been more customary. For this reason, the downloadable Excel grade charts on the book's website have been designed to accommodate either of the methods of grading that you may be required to use as a freelancer.

2 Access to current information

Accessing up-to-date information on sizing is a problem for freelancers and small companies as information from recent size surveys and research is not freely available.

Seminars, such as the ASBCI sizing seminars, can be very helpful for freelancers researching sizing and sizing issues. DVDs of the seminars are also available to buy from ASBCI. The ASBCI seminars on sizing that I have attended were up to date and informative. Industry experts spoke at both seminars and three types of body scanner were exhibited at one seminar. I learnt how each uses a different method to measure the body; I tried one out and was shown an example of the type of information that they are able to give.

A simple way to research current sizes and 'to fit' body measurements for the UK is to look for information freely available in the public domain. You should compare the sizes that companies are currently offering. It is important to update your research on a regular basis. You will not get individual increments other than basic chest, waist and hips (see Section 12.7) but it can help with measurements such as leg or skirt lengths.

Men's, women's and children's size charts are available in pattern cutting and grading books. It is wise to invest in the latest editions for the most recent size charts. Do not use outdated charts. The books with size charts that I find very useful are listed in Section 12.12.

For information on different countries' garment sizes, you could compare size charts freely available in the public domain, in catalogues and on the Internet. Figure 12.1 can be used as a guide to women's sizes for the UK, Europe, the USA and Japan. Remember individual sizes and measurements can vary, sometimes considerably, for individual brands, whichever country they come from. If you are developing a range which is to be sold both in the UK and overseas, you will need

Basic Women's Conversion Chart (using 8-size chart with 1 grade)										
size	XXS	XS	S	M	L	XL	XXL	XXXL	inc	
approx UK size	6	8	10	12	14	16	18	20	2	
approx European size	34	36	38	40	42	44	46	48	2	
approx American size	4	6	8	10	12	14	16	18	2	
approx Australian size	8	10	12	14	16	18	20	22	2	
approx Japanese size	7	9	11	13	15	17	19	21	2	
'To fit' body measurements										

This chart is to be used as a guide only. Any similarity to any other chart is coincidental. The author and publisher do not accept any liability.

Figure 12.1   Basic international women's sizes conversion chart

to explain to your client that there is no internationally accepted sizing system. They will need to adopt their own sizing and be prepared to give measurements to international buyers in addition to 'equivalent' sizes.

For downloadable template Excel charts, see Sections 12.10 and 12.11. The templates can be used to make your own charts.

3 Why sizing is different for different companies

Any one size, for example women's size 12, can be slightly or considerably different for individual companies. Some tend to size generously to make consumers feel better about their size as this may affect their decision to buy. Consumer expectations may not be realistic where size is concerned; people often do not recognise their actual body size, hence the tendency for 'vanity sizing'. Garments do need to fit consistently within a brand to give the consumer confidence that they will fit into the same size each time they buy. They may well gravitate towards the same brands after the initial attraction of the garment style due to the fit.

On the same day, I bought four garments, two stated a size larger on the label than the others, yet all four fitted me perfectly.

Some larger companies offer a variety of different 'fits' to try to accommodate differing body shapes, sizes and age groups. Once the target customer has been identified the type of fit can be decided. For example, a young female fashion range would have a different size chart from a range aimed at an older women's age group. The former may well be for a slimmer body shape; the latter for a fuller, more womanly body shape. Fashion attitude might dictate the brand a consumer chooses to buy from but fit can affect the final choice.

> "I have discovered over the past few years that smaller retailers and some brands tend to size their products on a slightly larger scale. One of the main reasons for this is to try to avoid large quantities of customer returns, especially in more fashionable womenswear. Another reason is that these companies may not have technical or qualified professional staff who have the knowledge to prepare size specifications. Therefore, the company will perhaps use specs from their manufacturers and slightly adjust them in order to 'personalise' these size charts as their own."
>
> David Robertson, Scullerthorpe

4 Charts for specific sizing issues

'Plus' size charts

It is important to remember that many plus sizes are for men and women of average height, therefore this needs to be a consideration when compiling plus size charts. Remember that it is not just the chest, waist and hips that increase with body size and weight; consider the tops of the arms and thighs and any other areas that can increase.

It is common to have larger increments between plus sizes, for example 6 cm (2 3/8"), 7.5cm (3") or even 10cm (4"). Sometimes two increment columns may be needed (e.g. on adult unisex charts); for example 7.5cm (3") could be used between the smaller sizes and 15cm (6") for very large sizes.

One company I worked for who included plus sizes in their ranges called their sizes 1, 2, 3, 4 and 5. Size 2 was about a UK 14–16 and size 5 about a UK 26–28. Increments of 10cm (4") were used between all sizes. Calling a garment 4XL or size 28 can be very off-putting and demoralising to consumers.

Children's unisex 'plus' charts are bigger on the chest, waist and hips than standard children's charts. When compiling charts, it is also important to consider other areas that can increase with size, such as the tops of the arms and thighs.

Tall and petite sizes

Garments for tall or petite men and women have different proportions. The shoulder length, armhole depth, chest/bust and hip height position, nape-to-waist, waist-to-hem, sleeve length, body rise and inside leg measurements will all be different. They all need to be considered and adjusted accordingly.

Undertake your own research in this area and compare measurements freely available in the public domain.

Maternity size charts

When designing maternity wear it is important to consider the changing body shape and other areas that are likely to increase in size in addition to the waistline. Michele Walker, a registered midwife for 32 years, explains some of the changes that take place during pregnancy:

> Although we know that weight gain should be 12.5kg, some people will gain considerably more than this; underweight women may gain significantly less. Weight gain is usually around the abdomen, breasts and thighs; the top of the arms may increase too. Of the average weight gain in pregnancy, which is 28lb (12.5kg), extra fluid in the body accounts for 1.2kg; breasts weigh an extra 0.4kg; storage of fat is about 4kg, the baby weighs 2.5 to 3.5kg; and the placenta weighs 0.5kg.

Women who are four months pregnant are very different in size and shape to those nearing full term so, obviously, it is difficult to accommodate them with well-fitting garments throughout their entire pregnancy. During the early months, women may simply find a size bigger sufficient and may not need maternity garments until later in their pregnancy. Maternity wear then sees them through to full term and often the first few weeks after giving birth as well. Designers also need to consider a pregnant woman's posture; as their abdomen gets bigger they tend to lean backwards and standard garments begin to be too short at the front hem. Maternity garments are cut longer at the front to accommodate the expanding abdomen.

'To fit' maternity size charts need to give the consumer a guide of which size to buy by giving pre-pregnancy measurements. To aid the customer in their selection, it would be wise to include on charts the information that a size larger may need to be chosen with an above average weight gain.

5 Creating Excel size charts

As a freelance designer, you may be asked or required to compile size and grade charts for first samples, first sample size sets and even for production. If you do not feel confident to do them yourself, consider recommending that your client employ a specialist in this area to undertake them or even sub-contract to a specialist yourself.

If you do intend to compile size and grading charts, ensure you keep up to date with research in this area. A wise investment would be to buy comprehensive specialist grading books to aid you in this area.

Excel grade charts look professional and can make your life easier by calculating grade increments and measurements. They are also easy to use, alter and amend.

'To fit' size charts

I have often been employed not only to design a range but also to resolve clients' sizing issues. I have found this to be an area that continues to be a problem for many companies.

Discuss with your client the specific size charts to which they require you to work. They may not have one, but just have a rather vague idea of what their sizes are. It is advisable to establish a 'to fit' body measurement size chart that is acceptable early on in the project, possibly adapting and accommodating their existing sizes.

Consider the sizes your client currently runs and what is successful, what is not and what the problem areas are. Confirm sizes and body shapes of target consumers the garments need to fit and create a 'to fit' size chart giving body measurements. Ensure you make very clear the fact that these charts are 'to fit' body measurements and not garment measurements, which will be individual to each garment due to fashion, fit, style and fabric. Clients may need to use the charts for publication in catalogues and they must be accurate and consistent. They can be accompanied by information about how to accurately obtain body measurements for the consumer.

Figure 12.2 is an example of a women's 'to fit' body measurements chart with a different set of grade increments for each size in the 'inc' columns. It can be used as a guide to making your own 'to fit' body measurement chart. A single grade chart could use many grade increment columns depending on individual sizing requirements. For a downloadable Excel template 'to fit' size chart, see Section 12.10.

Garment size charts

For a downloadable Excel template garment size chart, see Section 12.11. See Section 11.7 for full details of how to create detailed garment specification charts to accompany your Excel grade charts. The downloadable size chart templates can be used for

Basic Classic Women's Size Chart (8 sizes with individual grade increments)																
size	XXS		XS		S		M		L		XL		XXL		XXXL	
approx UK size	6	inc	8	inc	10	inc	12	inc	14	inc	16	inc	18	inc	20	
to fit bust – cms	78	4	82	4	86	4	90	5	95	6	101	6	107	6	113	cms
to fit bust – inches	31	1.5	32.5	1.5	34	1.4	35.4	2	37.4	2.4	39.8	2.4	42.2	2.4	44.6	ins
to fit waist – cms	61	4	65	4	69	4	73	5	78	6	84	6	90	6	96	cms
to fit waist – inches	24	1.5	25.5	1.5	27	1.5	28.5	2	30.5	2.4	32.9	2.4	35.3	2.4	37.7	ins
to fit hip – cms	86	4	90	4	94	4	98	5	103	6	109	6	115	6	121	cms
to fit hip – inches	34	1.5	35.5	1.5	37	1.5	38.5	2	40.5	2.4	42.9	2.4	45.3	2.4	47.7	ins
'To fit' body measurements																

This chart is to be used as a guide only. Any similarity to any other chart is coincidental. The author and publisher do not accept any liability.

Figure 12.2   Basic women's 'to fit' body measurements chart

women's, men's, girls', boys' and unisex garments. The increments and tolerances on the charts may be altered to suit individual requirements. There are three types of downloadable chart: one with an increment column between individual sizes, one with a single increment column and one with two increment columns. These template charts are intended to fulfil the variety of methods that a freelancer may be asked to use when compiling size charts for clients. The charts include up to eight sizes in separate columns. For sizes that are not required when using a chart, you can simply colour the text white or hide the columns. The column is still there but not visible. Colouring the text white or hiding it can also be used for rows that are not required. You can then make a PDF for the client showing only the required sizes and measurements. Figures 11.20 and 11.21 show example garment Excel charts.

6 Flat measurements

The example garment charts illustrated use mostly flat half-garment measurements; for these the tape measure is used flat on top of the garment. Some measurements, such as armholes, or the neck, are curved measurements. To achieve them, carefully bend the tape measure on its edge around the curve for accuracy.

Before measuring, gently shake the garment and lay it smooth and flat, without pulling or stretching, on a tabletop onto which the entire garment fits. Ensure the garment is relaxed, fastenings are closed and pleats lie flat or are pinned in position. Measurements that need to be taken stretched (i.e. elasticated parts) must be stated on the size chart clearly. Note that only the elastic can stretch, not the fabric.

During my own early years in manufacturing, a senior technologist showed me a method of measuring the 'across chest/bust' measurement for woven blouses that gives a more accurate bust measurement, as opposed to laying the tape straight across the flat garment. The particular garment that I was measuring was a conventional ladies' shirt-style blouse with bust darts. As the bust darts created fullness on the woven fabric, she demonstrated how the garment should be folded at a specified point below the armhole (that is, 2.5cm below the armhole point). When the garment is folded in this manner, there tends to be a slight curve and the measuring tape (using the tape measure on its edge for accuracy) should be used around the outer edge of the curve. This will give a more accurate bust measurement, as opposed to laying the tape straight across the garment.

David Robertson, Scullerthorpe

Size charts need to state clearly exactly where a measurement is taken from and too (for example, 2.5cm below the armhole for chest measurements) and the points to and from which measurements are taken. Take, for example, the higher neck point (HNP). The HNP must be indicated on illustrations for tops, jackets, dresses, etc. (see Figure 11.18). When taking measurements across the front or back of a garment, you need to state on the Excel chart the distance from the point at which these measurements are taken to the HNP. For example, in Figure 11.20, rows C, D, F and M give measurements with respect to HNP.

7 Grade increments

Grade increments are the amount of either increase or decrease in measurement between garment sizes. A grade increment is specified in millimetres, centimetres, inches or fractions of an inch. For larger sizes, garment measurements are 'graded up' (increased); for smaller sizes, they are 'graded down' (reduced).

More recent methods of grading have different increments between individual sizes. This is derived from research using body scanners for size surveys (see Sections 12.1 and 12.2). More traditional methods of grading may use only one set of grade increments between all sizes (see Figure 11.20) or, for example, unisex or plus sizes may have two sets of grade increments: a 1-grade increment (one size, 5cm/2" chest) between the smaller sizes then a 1.5-grade increment (one and a half sizes, 7.5cm/3") between the larger sizes (see Figure 11.21).

Children's size charts can have different grade increments between the sizes or just one grade between no more than two or three sizes to accommodate growth. Children's height and age is generally used as a guide to the consumer, though this is not always an accurate method. Consumers really need to know what body measurements a garment is designed to fit therefore it is wise to add a 'to fit' chest or waist measurement to children's size charts.

Individual companies may have their own grade increments that work for their garments that they ask you to use. Each garment design and grade needs to be specific and individual, although once you have worked out your grades for a company to fit their target customer, a system is likely to emerge.

It is wise to research and seek advice from an expert in grading, then create grade charts following and using grade rules/increments which makes sizing much easier.

Grade increments can be found or worked out from size charts in grading or pattern-cutting books. Some show the increments in a column at one side. Others do not and with those you need to work out the individual grades between sizes yourself. Be aware that increments between sizes may not be the same for each measurement.

Basic increments tend to be fairly standard in the industry. For example, chest, waist and hip measurements tend to have 5cm between grades. Be aware that some books use 4cm between chest, waist and hip and therefore all the other increments, such as shoulder, bicep, body rise, etc., will be different from those using a 5cm grade. If you compare several different size charts, you will find that they differ in some measurements and yet tend to be similar in others. You may find that not all charts have every measurement that you need, such as inside leg, underarm or thigh, so it is wise to have several different charts to hand.

Grade difficulties can be caused by design details, for example, in low-waisted trousers. Books give the body rise measurement from the natural waist, so you need to work out how much below the natural waistline the garment sits and then work out the correct percentage for the grade. If the front rise were to be dropped lower than the back, which would prevent trousers showing too much flesh when the wearer is bending, the grade for the front rise would be smaller than for the back. Again you would need to carefully work out the correct percentage for that particular grade.

Designers need to be very careful when compiling size charts and grading as incorrect grading can prove expensive. I was employed to correct some size charts for a company whose shoulder and arm length grades had been calculated incorrectly and had turned out far too long. The general fit on some garments was also poor and needed improvement. For another job, for a different company, I corrected the size and grade problems that had been created by someone untrained in this field.

8 Pre-production sampling and size sets

One company I was working for had not been sampling as I had advised. They had just gone straight into production. Fortunately, nothing had gone wrong but the chances are that something would at some stage.

Always recommend to clients in writing that a sample garment for each new style needs to be made in the correct fabric and checked for fit, size and style. Size charts can then be altered if necessary. A complete size set of samples should then be made and each size checked for fit and size. Be sure to state (preferably in writing) that should a client disregard your instructions it is at their own risk. Sometimes companies try to reduce costs by not spending the time and money necessary for sampling, but it is an essential process that ensures garments fit well and are graded correctly.

It is important to ensure that a 'sealing sample' (i.e. a sample garment, fabric, trimmings and the agreed size for production) and the correct size chart, including grades, are signed off by the client and agreed between all parties involved (which includes the client, the manufacturer and suppliers) before production goes ahead. This can prevent disputes with production at a later date. It is wise to ensure this is confirmed and dated in writing.

9 Tolerance

Tolerance is the acceptable variation of measurement for production garments that are made from a single size chart. This means, for example, that a number of size 14 garments in the same design may vary in measurement slightly, either larger or smaller than the size chart, but must be within the acceptable tolerance limit for each measurement. In Figure 11.20, for example, the tolerance (TOL +/−) for the measurement in row A is given as 1cm. Be aware of how different fabrics perform, there is not much 'give' in woven fabrics but care should be taken with stretch fabrics such as jersey.

10 Creating a 'to fit' body measurement size chart

Download the 'to fit' templates for a single grade (Figure 12.3) or individual grades for each size (Figure 12.4) from the book's website.

Basic 8-Size Chart with 1 Grade Increment										
size										
approx UK size									inc	
to fit .... cms	-2	-1	0	1	2	3	4	5	1	cms
to fit .... inches	-2	-1	0	1	2	3	4	5	1	ins
to fit .... cms	-2	-1	0	1	2	3	4	5	1	cms
to fit .... inches	-2	-1	0	1	2	3	4	5	1	ins
to fit .... cms	-2	-1	0	1	2	3	4	5	1	cms
to fit .... inches	-2	-1	0	1	2	3	4	5	1	ins
'To fit' body measurements										

This chart is to be used as a guide only. Any similarity to any other chart is coincidental. The author and publisher do not accept any liability.

Figure 12.3 Template for 'to fit' eight-size chart with one grade increment

Basic 8-Size Chart with Individual Grade Increments															
size															
approx UK size		inc		inc		inc		inc		inc		inc		inc	
to fit .... cms	-2	1	-1	1	0	1	1	1	2	1	3	1	4	1	5	cms
to fit .... inches	-2	1	-1	1	0	1	1	1	2	1	3	1	4	1	5	ins
to fit .... cms	-2	1	-1	1	0	1	1	1	2	1	3	1	4	1	5	cms
to fit .... inches	-2	1	-1	1	0	1	1	1	2	1	3	1	4	1	5	ins
to fit .... cms	-2	1	-1	1	0	1	1	1	2	1	3	1	4	1	5	cms
to fit .... inches	-2	1	-1	1	0	1	1	1	2	1	3	1	4	1	5	ins
'To fit' body measurements															

This chart is to be used as a guide only, any similarities to any other chart is coincidental, the author & publisher does not accept any liability.

Figure 12.4 Template for 'to fit' eight-size chart with individual grade increments

Rename the charts you download and enter the following information into the appropriate cells:

- chart name;
- client's name for the size (e.g. S, M, L);
- approximate UK size (10, 12, 14, etc.) or European size (38, 42, 44, etc.);
- the body area to which the size pertains (column A, e.g. 'to fit bust cms').

Enter the correct body measurements into the grey column (column D in Figure 12.3 and column F in Figure 12.4). For each row, enter the correct grade increments (column J in Figure 12.3 and columns C, E, G, I, K, M and O in Figure 12.4). The chart will automatically calculate the sizes, check to ensure that it is calculating correctly. Use the formulas in Figure 12.5 as a guide to check Figure 12.3 and the formulas in Figure 12.6 to check Figure 12.4. When you click on a cell, its formula shows in the formula bar.

Note: It is important to familiarise yourself with the charts, so first download a sample chart and experiment with it to see how it works. If you find it difficult, read the Excel instruction manual or consider taking a course in Excel.

Basic 8-Size Chart with 1 Grade Increment											
size											
approx UK size										inc	
to fit .... cms	=+C4-$J4	=+D4-$J4		=+D4+J4	=+E4+J4	=+F4+J4	=+G4+J4	=+H4+J4			cms
to fit .... inches	=+C5-$J5	=+D5-$J5		=+D5+J5	=+E5+J5	=+F5+J5	=+G5+J5	=+H5+J5			ins
to fit .... cms	=+C6-$J6	=+D6-$J6		=+D6+J6	=+E6+J6	=+F6+J6	=+G6+J6	=+H6+J6			cms
to fit .... inches	=+C7-$J7	=+D7-$J7		=+D7+J7	=+E7+J7	=+F7+J7	=+G7+J7	=+H7+J7			ins
to fit .... cms	=+C8-$J8	=+D8-$J8		=+D8+J8	=+E8+J8	=+F8+J8	=+G8+J8	=+H8+J8			cms
to fit .... inches	=+C9-$J9	=+D9-$J9		=+D9+J9	=+E9+J9	=+F9+J9	=+G9+J9	=+H9+J9			ins
'To fit' body measurements											

This chart is to be used as a guide only. Any similarity to any other chart is coincidental. The author and publisher do not accept any liability.

☐ format cells = general

Figure 12.5   Formulas for basic eight-size chart with one grade increment

Basic 8-Size Chart with Individual Grade Increments														
size														
approx UK size		inc		inc		inc		inc		inc		inc		inc
to fit .... cms	=+D4-C4		=+F4-E4			=+F4+G4		=+H4+I4		=+J4+K4		=+L4+M4		=+N4+O4	cms
to fit .... inches	=+D5-C5		=+F5-E5			=+F5+G5		=+H5+I5		=+J5+K5		=+L5+M5		=+N5+O5	ins
to fit .... cms	=+D6-C6		=+F6-E6			=+F6+G6		=+H6+I6		=+J6+K6		=+L6+M6		=+N6+O6	cms
to fit .... inches	=+D7-C7		=+F7-E7			=+F7+G7		=+H7+I7		=+J7+K7		=+L7+M7		=+N7+O7	ins
to fit .... cms	=+D8-C8		=+F8-E8			=+F8+G8		=+H8+I8		=+J8+K8		=+L8+M8		=+N8+O8	cms
to fit .... inches	=+D9-C9		=+F9-E9			=+F9+G9		=+H9+I9		=+J9+K9		=+L9+M9		=+N9+O9	ins
'To fit' body measurements														

This chart is to be used as a guide only. Any similarity to any other chart is coincidental. The author and publisher do not accept any liability.

☐ format cells = general

Figure 12.6   Formulas for basic eight-size chart with individual grade increments

11 Creating a garment size chart

Download the appropriate template from the book's website:

- an eight-size, individual-grade chart (Figure 12.7);
- an eight-size, one-grade chart (Figure 12.8);
- an eight-size, two-grade chart (Figure 12.9).

All Excel garment grade charts need a detailed garment specification sheet as described in Section 11.7.

The empty columns next to each measurement column (e.g. columns D and F in Figure 12.8) are for corrections or notes that may need to be made at any stage during the development process or to compare sample measurements when sample garments are checked against the original chart at a later date.

To use the charts, enter the following information into the appropriate cells at the top of the chart:

- style number or code;
- description;
- brand;
- season;
- fabric;
- trim;
- date;
- description of grade (men's, ladies or children's);
- the name of each measurement that matches the label (A–Z) on the detailed specification (into column B);
- acceptable tolerances in the TOL +/− column.

Enter the following information into the appropriate rows:

- the 'to fit' information for chest/bust, size or height in inches;
- the 'to fit' information for chest/bust, size or height in cm;
- the size (e.g. UK size 10, 12, 14; chest measurement; or approximate age) – note that for sizes that are not numeric (e.g. S, M, L), you must type the sizes directly into the cell at the top of each column;
- the correct body measurement (A–Z) that matches the detailed specification.

For the reference size, enter the garment measurements into the grey column (column G in Figure 12.8).

Enter the correct grade increment for each body measurement (column S in Figure 12.8).

The chart then automatically calculates the sizes.

8-Size Chart with Individual Grades

Style no:	Season:		Date:
Description:	Fabric:		Grade:
Brand:	Trim:		Grade:

	-3	GRADE INC	-2	GRADE INC	-1	GRADE INC	0	GRADE INC	1	GRADE INC	4	inches	TOL +/-
To fit .... inches	-3 ins	1	-2 ins	1	-1 ins	1	0 ins	1	1 ins	1	4	ins	
To fit .... cms	-3 cms	1	-2 cms	1	-1 cms	1	0 cms	1	1 cms	1	4	cms	
UK size	-3	1	-2	1	-1	1	0	1	1	1	4		TOL +/-
A	-3	1	-2	1	-1	1	0	1	1	1	2		cms
B	-3	1	-2	1	-1	1	0	1	1	1	2		cms
C	-3	1	-2	1	-1	1	0	1	1	1	2		cms
D	-3	1	-2	1	-1	1	0	1	1	1	2		cms
E	-3	1	-2	1	-1	1	0	1	1	1	2		cms
F	-3	1	-2	1	-1	1	0	1	1	1	2		cms
G	-3	1	-2	1	-1	1	0	1	1	1	2		cms
H	-3	1	-2	1	-1	1	0	1	1	1	2		cms
I	-3	1	-2	1	-1	1	0	1	1	1	2		cms
J	-3	1	-2	1	-1	1	0	1	1	1	2		cms
K	-3	1	-2	1	-1	1	0	1	1	1	2		cms
L	-3	1	-2	1	-1	1	0	1	1	1	2		cms
M	-3	1	-2	1	-1	1	0	1	1	1	2		cms
N	-3	1	-2	1	-1	1	0	1	1	1	2		cms
O	-3	1	-2	1	-1	1	0	1	1	1	2		cms
P	-3	1	-2	1	-1	1	0	1	1	1	2		cms
Q	-3	1	-2	1	-1	1	0	1	1	1	2		cms
R	-3	1	-2	1	-1	1	0	1	1	1	2		cms
S	-3	1	-2	1	-1	1	0	1	1	1	2		cms
T	-3	1	-2	1	-1	1	0	1	1	1	2		cms
U	-3	1	-2	1	-1	1	0	1	1	1	2		cms
V	-3	1	-2	1	-1	1	0	1	1	1	2		cms
W	-3	1	-2	1	-1	1	0	1	1	1	2		cms
X	-3	1	-2	1	-1	1	0	1	1	1	2		cms
Y	-3	1	-2	1	-1	1	0	1	1	1	2		cms
Z	-3	1	-2	1	-1	1	0	1	1	1	2		cms

garment measurements

This chart is to be used as a guide only. Any similarity to any other chart is coincidental. The author and publisher do not accept any liability.

Figure 12.7 Template for eight-size garment chart with individual grade increments (columns R–W are hidden so that you can see the right of the spreadsheet)

156

8-Size Chart with 1 Grade

Style no:		Season:		Date:
Description:		Fabric:		Grade:
Brand:		Trim:		

	-2		-1		0		1		2		3		4		5		GRADE INC		TOL +/-
To fit ………… inches	**-2**	ins	**-1**	ins		ins	**1**	ins	**2**	ins	**3**	ins	**4**	ins	**5**	ins	**inches**		
To fit ………… cms	**-2**	cms	**-1**	cms		cms	**1**	cms	**2**	cms	**3**	cms	**4**	cms	**5**	cms	**cms**		
UK size	**-2**		**-1**		**0**		**1**		**2**		**3**		**4**		**5**		*1*		TOL +/-
A	-2		-1		0		1		2		3		4		5		*1*		cms
B	-2		-1		0		1		2		3		4		5		*1*		cms
C	-2		-1		0		1		2		3		4		5		*1*		cms
D	-2		-1		0		1		2		3		4		5		*1*		cms
E	-2		-1		0		1		2		3		4		5		*1*		cms
F	-2		-1		0		1		2		3		4		5		*1*		cms
G	-2		-1		0		1		2		3		4		5		*1*		cms
H	-2		-1		0		1		2		3		4		5		*1*		cms
I	-2		-1		0		1		2		3		4		5		*1*		cms
J	-2		-1		0		1		2		3		4		5		*1*		cms
K	-2		-1		0		1		2		3		4		5		*1*		cms
L	-2		-1		0		1		2		3		4		5		*1*		cms
M	-2		-1		0		1		2		3		4		5		*1*		cms
N	-2		-1		0		1		2		3		4		5		*1*		cms
O	-2		-1		0		1		2		3		4		5		*1*		cms
P	-2		-1		0		1		2		3		4		5		*1*		cms
Q	-2		-1		0		1		2		3		4		5		*1*		cms
R	-2		-1		0		1		2		3		4		5		*1*		cms
S	-2		-1		0		1		2		3		4		5		*1*		cms
T	-2		-1		0		1		2		3		4		5		*1*		cms
U	-2		-1		0		1		2		3		4		5		*1*		cms
V	-2		-1		0		1		2		3		4		5		*1*		cms
W	-2		-1		0		1		2		3		4		5		*1*		cms
X	-2		-1		0		1		2		3		4		5		*1*		cms
Y	-2		-1		0		1		2		3		4		5		*1*		cms
Z	-2		-1		0		1		2		3		4		5		*1*		cms

garment measurements

This chart is to be used as a guide only. Any similarity to any other chart is coincidental. The author and publisher do not accept any liability.

Figure 12.8 Template for eight-size garment chart with one grade increment

157

8-Size Chart with 2 Grades

Style no:		Season:		Date:	
Description:		Fabric:			
Brand:		Trim:		Grade:	

	To fit .... inches											GRADE INC				TOL +/-
	To fit .... cms															
UK size	-3	-2	-1	0	1	1.5	3	4.5	6		1.5				
	ins	ins	ins	ins	ins	ins	ins	ins	ins		inches				
	cms	cms	cms	cms	cms	cms	cms	cms	cms		cms				
A	-3	-2	-1	0	1	1.5	3	4.5	6		1.5	cms
B	-3	-2	-1	0	1	1.5	3	4.5	6		1.5	cms
C	-3	-2	-1	0	1	1.5	3	4.5	6		1.5	cms
D	-3	-2	-1	0	1	1.5	3	4.5	6		1.5	cms
E	-3	-2	-1	0	1	1.5	3	4.5	6		1.5	cms
F	-3	-2	-1	0	1	1.5	3	4.5	6		1.5	cms
G	-3	-2	-1	0	1	1.5	3	4.5	6		1.5	cms
H	-3	-2	-1	0	1	1.5	3	4.5	6		1.5	cms
I	-3	-2	-1	0	1	1.5	3	4.5	6		1.5	cms
J	-3	-2	-1	0	1	1.5	3	4.5	6		1.5	cms
K	-3	-2	-1	0	1	1.5	3	4.5	6		1.5	cms
L	-3	-2	-1	0	1	1.5	3	4.5	6		1.5	cms
M	-3	-2	-1	0	1	1.5	3	4.5	6		1.5	cms
N	-3	-2	-1	0	1	1.5	3	4.5	6		1.5	cms
O	-3	-2	-1	0	1	1.5	3	4.5	6		1.5	cms
P	-3	-2	-1	0	1	1.5	3	4.5	6		1.5	cms
Q	-3	-2	-1	0	1	1.5	3	4.5	6		1.5	cms
R	-3	-2	-1	0	1	1.5	3	4.5	6		1.5	cms
S	-3	-2	-1	0	1	1.5	3	4.5	6		1.5	cms
T	-3	-2	-1	0	1	1.5	3	4.5	6		1.5	cms
U	-3	-2	-1	0	1	1.5	3	4.5	6		1.5	cms
V	-3	-2	-1	0	1	1.5	3	4.5	6		1.5	cms
W	-3	-2	-1	0	1	1.5	3	4.5	6		1.5	cms
X	-3	-2	-1	0	1	1.5	3	4.5	6		1.5	cms
Y	-3	-2	-1	0	1	1.5	3	4.5	6		1.5	cms
Z	-3	-2	-1	0	1	1.5	3	4.5	6		1.5	cms

garment measurements

This chart is to be used as a guide only. Any similarity to any other chart is coincidental. The author and publisher do not accept any liability.

Figure 12.9 Template for eight-size garment chart with two grade increments

158

To enter specific values (e.g. one length of zip (say 15cm) for smaller sizes and one length (say 20cm) for larger sizes), enter the measurements directly into the cells to override the formulas.

Change the text colour for any rows or columns that you are not using to white so that they cannot be seen.

If you need to add an extra row to your chart, click on the chart where the row is required. On the menu, select Insert, Rows. You need to add the formulas to any new rows, so it may be simpler to copy and paste an empty row that contains the formulas. Then double-check all formulas in the worksheet. You need to amend the information in the altered rows and any other rows your alterations have affected.

Remember: Double-check your charts to ensure they are calculating correctly each time you use them. Use Figures 12.10, 12.11 and 12.12 as a guide to the correct formulas and cell formats to ensure that they are working correctly. When you click on a cell its formula will show in the formula bar.

Charts can be altered and amended by altering the garment measurements in the grey column or increments in the increment columns.

Note: It is important to familiarise yourself with the charts. Download a sample chart and experiment with it to see how it works. If you find it difficult, read the Excel instruction manual or consider taking a course in Excel.

			8-Size Chart with Individual Grades								
Style no:			Season:								
Description:			Fabric:								
Brand:			Trim:								
				GRADE INC			GRADE INC			GRADE INC	
	To fit .... inches		=+F7-$E7	ins		=+I7-$H7	ins		=+L7-$K7	ins	0
	To fit .... cms		=+F8-$E8	cms		=+I8-$H8	cms		=+L8-$K8	cms	0
	UK size		=+F9-$E9			=+I9-$H9			=+L9-$K9		0
A			=+F11-$E11			=+I11-$H11			=+L11-$K11		0
B			=+F12-$E12			=+I12-$H12			=+EL12-$K12		0
C			=+F13-$E13			=+I13-$H13			=+L13-$K13		0
D			=+F14-$E14			=+I14-$H14			=+L14-$K14		0
E			=+F15-$E15			=+I15-$H15			=+L15-$K15		0
F			=+F16-$E16			=+I16-$H16			=+L16-$K16		0
G			=+F17-$E17			=+I17-$H17			=+L17-$K17		0
H			=+F18-$E18			=+I18-$H18			=+L18-$K18		0
I			=+F19-$E19			=+I19-$H19			=+L19-$K19		0
J			=+F20-$E20			=+I20-$H20			=+L20-$K20		0
K			=+F21-$E21			=+I21-$H21			=+L21-$K21		0
L			=+F22-$E22			=+I22-$H22			=+L22-$K22		0
M			=+F23-$E23			=+I23-$H23			=+L23-$K23		0
N			=+F24-$E24			=+I24-$H24			=+L24-$K24		0
O			=+F25-$E25			=+I25-$H25			=+L25-$K25		0
P			=+F26-$E26			=+I26-$H26			=+L26-$K26		0
Q			=+F27-$E27			=+I27-$H27			=+L27-$K27		0
R			=+F28-$E28			=+I28-$H28			=+L28-$K28		0
S			=+F29-$E29			=+I29-$29			=+L29-$K29		0
T			=+F30-$E30			=+I30-$H30			=+L30-$K30		0
U			=+F31-$E31			=+I31-$H31			=+L31-$K31		0
V			=+F32-$E32			=+I32-$H32			=+L32-$K32		0
W			=+F33-$E33			=+I33-$H33			=+L33-$K33		0
X			=+F34-$E34			=+I34-$H34			=+L34-$K34		0
Y			=+F35-$E35			=+I35-$H35			=+L35-$K35		0
Z			=+F36-$E36			=+I36-$H36			=+L36-$K36		0

garment measurements

This chart is to be used as a guide only. Any similarity to any other chart is coincidental. The author and publisher do not accept any liability.

format cells = general

Figure 12.10 Formulas for eight-size garment chart with individual grade increments

	Date:	
	Grade:	

	GRADE INC			GRADE INC			GRADE INC			GRADE INC			
ins	=+L7+$N7	ins		=+O7+$Q7	ins		=+R7+$T7	ins		=+U7+$W7	ins	inches	
cms	=+L8+$N8	cms		=+O8+$Q8	cms		=+R8+$T8	cms		=+U8+$W8	cms	cms	
	=+L9+$N9			=+O9+$Q9			=+R9+$T9			=+U9+$W9			
												TOL +/-	
	=+L11+$N11			−+O11+$Q11			−+R11+$T11			=+U11+$W11			cms
	=+L12+$N12			=+OL12+$Q12			=+RL12+$T12			=+U12+$W12			cms
	=+L13+$N13			=+O13+$Q13			=+R13+$T13			=+U13+$W13			cms
	=+L14+$N14			=+O14+$Q14			=+R14+$T14			=+U14+$W14			cms
	=+L15+$N15			=+O15+$Q15			=+R15+$T15			=+U15+$W15			cms
	=+L16+$N16			=+O16+$Q16			=+R16+$T16			=+U16+$W16			cms
	=+L17+$N17			=+O17+$Q17			=+R17+$T17			=+U17+$W17			cms
	=+L18+$N18			=+O18+$Q18			=+R18+$T18			=+U18+$W18			cms
	=+L19+$N19			=+O19+$Q19			=+R19+$T19			=+U19+$W19			cms
	=+L20+$N20			=+O20+$Q20			=+R20+$T20			=+U20+$W20			cms
	=+L21+$N21			=+O21+$Q21			=+R21+$T21			=+U21+$W21			cms
	=+L22+$N22			=+O22+$Q22			=+R22+$T22			=+U22+$W22			cms
	=+L23+$N23			=+O23+$Q23			=+R23+$T23			=+U23+$W23			cms
	=+L24+$N24			=+O24+$Q24			=+R24+$T24			=+U24+$W24			cms
	=+L25+$N25			=+O25+$Q25			=+R25+$T25			=+U25+$W25			cms
	=+L26+$N26			=+O26+$Q26			=+R26+$T26			=+U26+$W26			cms
	=+L27+$N27			=+O27+$Q27			=+R27+$T27			=+U27+$W27			cms
	=+L28+$N28			=+O28+$Q28			=+R28+$T28			=+U28+$W28			cms
	=+L29+$N29			=+O29+$Q29			=+R29+$T29			=+U29+$W29			cms
	=+L30+$N30			=+O30+$Q30			=+R30+$T30			=+U30+$W30			cms
	=+L31+$N31			=+O31+$Q31			=+R31+$T31			=+U31+$W31			cms
	=+L32+$N32			=+O32+$Q32			=+R32+$T32			=+U32+$W32			cms
	=+L33+$N33			=+O33+$Q33			=+R33+$T33			=+U33+$W33			cms
	=+L34+$N34			=+O34+$Q34			=+R34+$T34			=+U34+$W34			cms
	=+L35+$N35			=+O35+$Q35			=+R35+$T35			=+U35+$W35			cms
	=+L36+$N36			=+O36+$Q36			=+R36+$T36			=+U36+$W36			cms

8-Size Chart with 1 Grade

Style no:	Season:		Date:
Description:	Fabric:		Grade:
Brand:	Trim:		

	To fit .... inches	To fit .... cms	UK size								GRADE INC	
	=+E5-$S5 =+E6-$S6 =+E7-$S7	=+G5-$S5 =+G6-$S6 =+G7-$S7	=+G5+$S5 =+G6+$S6 =+G7+$S7	=+I5-$S5 =+I6-$S6 =+I7-$S7	=+I5+$S5 =+I6+$S6 =+I7+$S7	=+K5-$S5 =+K6-$S6 =+K7-$S7	=+K5+$S5 =+K6+$S6 =+K7+$S7	=+M5-$S5 =+M6-$S6 =+M7-$S7	=+M5+$S5 =+M6+$S6 =+M7+$S7	=+O5+$S5 =+O6+$S6 =+O7+$S7	inches ins / cms	cms cms / TOL +/-

Size	=+E-$S	=+G-$S	=+G+$S	=+I-$S	=+I+$S	=+K-$S	=+K+$S	=+M-$S	=+M+$S	=+O+$S
A	=+E9-$S9	=+G9-$S9	=+G9+$S9	=+I9-$S9	=+I9+$S9	=+K9-$S9	=+K9+$S9	=+M9-$S9	=+M9+$S9	=+O9+$S9
B	=+E10-$S10	=+G10-$S10	=+G10+$S10	=+I10-$S10	=+I10+$S10	=+K10-$S10	=+K10+$S10	=+M10-$S10	=+M10+$S10	=+O10+$S10
C	=+E11-$S11	=+G11-$S11	=+G11+$S11	=+I11-$S11	=+I11+$S11	=+K11-$S11	=+K11+$S11	=+M11-$S11	=+M11+$S11	=+O11+$S11
D	=+E12-$S12	=+G12-$S12	=+G12+$S12	=+I12-$S12	=+I12+$S12	=+K12-$S12	=+K12+$S12	=+M12-$S12	=+M12+$S12	=+O12+$S12
E	=+E13-$S13	=+G13-$S13	=+G13+$S13	=+I13-$S13	=+I13+$S13	=+K13-$S13	=+K13+$S13	=+M13-$S13	=+M13+$S13	=+O13+$S13
F	=+E14-$S14	=+G14-$S14	=+G14+$S14	=+I14-$S14	=+I14+$S14	=+K14-$S14	=+K14+$S14	=+M14-$S14	=+M14+$S14	=+O14+$S14
G	=+E15-$S15	=+G15-$S15	=+G15+$S15	=+I15-$S15	=+I15+$S15	=+K15-$S15	=+K15+$S15	=+M15-$S15	=+M15+$S15	=+O15+$S15
H	=+E16-$S16	=+G16-$S16	=+G16+$S16	=+I16-$S16	=+I16+$S16	=+K16-$S16	=+K16+$S16	=+M16-$S16	=+M16+$S16	=+O16+$S16
I	=+E17-$S17	=+G17-$S17	=+G17+$S17	=+I17-$S17	=+I17+$S17	=+K17-$S17	=+K17+$S17	=+M17-$S17	=+M17+$S17	=+O17+$S17
J	=+E18-$S18	=+G18-$S18	=+G18+$S18	=+I18-$S18	=+I18+$S18	=+K18-$S18	=+K18+$S18	=+M18-$S18	=+M18+$S18	=+O18+$S18
K	=+E19-$S19	=+G19-$S19	=+G19+$S19	=+I19-$S19	=+I19+$S19	=+K19-$S19	=+K19+$S19	=+M19-$S19	=+M19+$S19	=+O19+$S19
L	=+E20-$S20	=+G20-$S20	=+G20+$S20	=+I20-$S20	=+I20+$S20	=+K20-$S20	=+K20+$S20	=+M20-$S20	=+M20+$S20	=+O20+$S20
M	=+E21-$S21	=+G21-$S21	=+G21+$S21	=+I21-$S21	=+I21+$S21	=+K21-$S21	=+K21+$S21	=+M21-$S21	=+M21+$S21	=+O21+$S21
N	=+E22-$S22	=+G22-$S22	=+G22+$S22	=+I22-$S22	=+I22+$S22	=+K22-$S22	=+K22+$S22	=+M22-$S22	=+M22+$S22	=+O22+$S22
O	=+E23-$S23	=+G23-$S23	=+G23+$S23	=+I23-$S23	=+I23+$S23	=+K23-$S23	=+K23+$S23	=+M23-$S23	=+M23+$S23	=+O23+$S23
P	=+E24-$S24	=+G24-$S24	=+G24+$S24	=+I24-$S24	=+I24+$S24	=+K24-$S24	=+K24+$S24	=+M24-$S24	=+M24+$S24	=+O24+$S24
Q	=+E25-$S25	=+G25-$S25	=+G25+$S25	=+I25-$S25	=+I25+$S25	=+K25-$S25	=+K25+$S25	=+M25-$S25	=+M25+$S25	=+O25+$S25
R	=+E26-$S26	=+G26-$S26	=+G26+$S26	=+I26-$S26	=+I26+$S26	=+K26-$S26	=+K26+$S26	=+M26-$S26	=+M26+$S26	=+O26+$S26
S	=+E27-$S27	=+G27-$S27	=+G27+$S27	=+I27-$S27	=+I27+$S27	=+K27-$S27	=+K27+$S27	=+M27-$S27	=+M27+$S27	=+O27+$S27
T	=+E28-$S28	=+G28-$S28	=+G28+$S28	=+I28-$S28	=+I28+$S28	=+K28-$S28	=+K28+$S28	=+M28-$S28	=+M28+$S28	=+O28+$S28
U	=+E29-$S29	=+G29-$S29	=+G29+$S29	=+I29-$S29	=+I29+$S29	=+K29-$S29	=+K29+$S29	=+M29-$S29	=+M29+$S29	=+O29+$S29
V	=+E30-$S30	=+G30-$S30	=+G30+$S30	=+I30-$S30	=+I30+$S30	=+K30-$S30	=+K30+$S30	=+M30-$S30	=+M30+$S30	=+O30+$S30
Y	=+E33-$S33	=+G33-$S33	=+G33+$S33	=+I33-$S33	=+I33+$S33	=+K33-$S33	=+K33+$S33	=+M33-$S33	=+M33+$S33	=+O33+$S33
Z	=+E34-$S34	=+G34-$S34	=+G34+$S34	=+I34-$S34	=+I34+$S34	=+K34-$S34	=+K34+$S34	=+M34-$S34	=+M34+$S34	=+O34+$S34

garment measurements

format cells = general

This chart is to be used as a guide only. Any similarity to any other chart is coincidental. The author and publisher do not accept any liability.

Figure 12.11 Formulas for eight-size garment chart with one grade increment

8-Size Chart with 2 Grades

Style no:	Season:	Date:
Description:	Fabric:	Grade:
Brand:	Trim:	

	To fit .... inches	ins	cms	ins	ins	GRADE INC		cms	cms	cms	
	=+E5-$K5	=+G5-$K5	=+I5-$K5				=+I5+$T5	=+L5+$T5	=+N5+$T5	=+P5+$T5	inches
	To fit .... cms =+E6-$K6	cms =+G6-$K6	=+I6-$K6	cms	cms		=+I6+$T6	=+L6+$T6	=+N6+$T6	=+P6+$T6	cms
	UK size =+E7-$K7	=+G7-$K7	=+I7-$K7				=+I7+$T7	=+L7+$T7	=+N7+$T7	=+P7+$T7	UK size
											TOL +/-
A	=+E9-$K9	=+G9-$K9	=+I9-$K9				=+I9+$T9	=+L9+$T9	=+N9+$T9	=+P9+$T9	cms
B	=+E10-$K10	=+G10-$K10	=+I10-$K10				=+I10+$T10	=+L10+$T10	=+N10+$T10	=+P10+$T10	cms
C	=+E11-$K11	=+G11-$K11	=+I11-$K11				=+I11+$T11	=+L11+$T11	=+N11+$T11	=+P11+$T11	cms
D	=+E12-$K12	=+G12-$K12	=+I12-$K12				=+I12+$T12	=+L12+$T12	=+N12+$T12	=+P12+$T12	cms
E	=+E13-$K13	=+G13-$K13	=+I13-$K13				=+I13+$T13	=+L13+$T13	=+N13+$T13	=+P13+$T13	cms
F	=+E14-$K14	=+G14-$K14	=+I14-$K14				=+I14+$T14	=+L14+$T14	=+N14+$T14	=+P14+$T14	cms
G	=+E15-$K15	=+G15-$K15	=+I15-$K15				=+I15+$T15	=+L15+$T15	=+N15+$T15	=+P15+$T15	cms
H	=+E16-$K16	=+G16-$K16	=+I16-$K16				=+I16+$T16	=+L16+$T16	=+N16+$T16	=+P16+$T16	cms
I	=+E17-$K17	=+G17-$K17	=+I17-$K17				=+I17+$T17	=+L17+$T17	=+N17+$T17	=+P17+$T17	cms
J	=+E18-$K18	=+G18-$K18	=+I18-$K18				=+I18+$T18	=+L18+$T18	=+N18+$T18	=+P18+$T18	cms
K	=+E19-$K19	=+G19-$K19	=+I19-$K19				=+I19+$T19	=+L19+$T19	=+N19+$T19	=+P19+$T19	cms
L	=+E20-$K20	=+G20-$K20	=+I20-$K20				=+I20+$T20	=+L20+$T20	=+N20+$T20	=+P20+$T20	cms
M	=+E21-$K21	=+G21-$K21	=+I21-$K21				=+I21+$T21	=+L21+$T21	=+N21+$T21	=+P21+$T21	cms
N	=+E22-$K22	=+G22-$K22	=+I22-$K22				=+I22+$T22	=+L22+$T22	=+N22+$T22	=+P22+$T22	cms
O	=+E23-$K23	=+G23-$K23	=+I23-$K23				=+I23+$T23	=+L23+$T23	=+N23+$T23	=+P23+$T23	cms
P	=+E24-$K24	=+G24-$K24	=+I24-$K24				=+I24+$T24	=+L24+$T24	=+N24+$T24	=+P24+$T24	cms
Q	=+E25-$K25	=+G25-$K25	=+I25-$K25				=+I25+$T25	=+L25+$T25	=+N25+$T25	=+P25+$T25	cms
R	=+E26-$K26	=+G26-$K26	=+I26-$K26				=+I26+$T26	=+L26+$T26	=+N26+$T26	=+P26+$T26	cms
S	=+E27-$K27	=+G27-$K27	=+I27-$K27				=+I27+$T27	=+L27+$T27	=+N27+$T27	=+P27+$T27	cms
T	=+E28-$K28	=+G28-$K28	=+I28-$K28				=+I28+$T28	=+L28+$T28	=+N28+$T28	=+P28+$T28	cms
U	=+E29-$K29	=+G29-$K29	=+I29-$K29				=+I29+$T29	=+L29+$T29	=+N29+$T29	=+P29+$T29	cms
V	=+E30-$K30	=+G30-$K30	=+I30-$K30				=+I30+$T30	=+L30+$T30	=+N30+$T30	=+P30+$T30	cms
Y	=+E33-$K33	=+G33-$K33	=+I33-$K33				=+I33+$T33	=+L33+$T33	=+N33+$T33	=+P33+$T33	cms
Z	=+E34-$K34	=+G34-$K34	=+I34-$K34				=+I34+$T34	=+L34+$T34	=+N34+$T34	=+P34+$T34	cms

garment measurements

format cells = general

This chart is to be used as a guide only. Any similarity to any other chart is coincidental. The author and publisher do not accept any liability.

Figure 12.12 Formulas for eight-size garment chart with two grade increments

163

12 References

Aldrich, W. (2006) *Metric Pattern Cutting for Menswear*, 5th Edition. John Wiley & Sons.

Aldrich, W. (2008) *Metric Pattern Cutting for Women's Wear*, 5th Edition. Blackwell Publishing.

Aldrich, W. (2009) *Metric Pattern Cutting for Children's Wear and Babywear*, 4th Edition. Blackwell Publishing.

Shoben, M. M. and Taylor, P. J. (2004) *Grading for the Fashion Industry: Theory and Practice*, 3rd Edition. LCFS Fashion Media.

Organisations and Useful Information

Organisations mentioned in the book

ASBCI Association of Suppliers to the British Clothing Industry brings together the clothing industry, from fibre manufacturers to garment manufacturers, retailers and people who provide aftercare. They hold regular technical seminars that tackle a variety of important industry topics.
Unit 5, 25 Square Road, Halifax, HX1 1QG. Telephone: +44 (0) 1422 354666. Email: office@asbci.co.uk. Website: www.asbci.co.uk.

Business Link. Helpline: 0845 600 9006. Website: www.businesslink.gov.uk.

Citizens' Advice Bureau. Website: www.citizensadvice.org.uk.

Department for Business, Innovation & Skills (BIS) through enterprise and business support, BIS sustain growth and higher skills across the economy and strengthens the enterprise environment for small businesses.
1 Victoria Street, London, SW1H 0ET. Telephone: +44 (0) 20 7215 5000. Email: enquiries@bis.gsi.gov.uk. Website: www.bis.gov.uk.

EMTEX Designer Forum supports clothing and textile students, lecturers, freelancers, companies, retailers and wholesalers throughout the UK. It has a trend library that members can use.
69–73, Lower Parliament Street, Nottingham, NG1 3BB. Telephone: +44 (0) 115 9115339. Email: enquiries@emtex.org.uk. Website: www.emtex.org.uk.

Health & Safety Executive (HSE). Website: www.hse.gov.uk/simple-health-safety.

HM Revenue & Customs (HMRC). Telephone: 0845 010 9000.
Website: www.hmrc.gov.uk.
Helpline for the newly self-employed: 0845 915 4515.
Self-Assessment Helpline: 0845 9000 444. Website: www.hmrc.gov.uk/sa.
VAT and Excise Helpline: 0845 010 9000. Website: www.hmrc.gov.uk/vat.

Learning and Skills Improvement Service (LSIS). Website: www.excellencegateway.org.uk/page.aspx?o=320146.

Mode Information Ltd provides creative trend forecasting, catwalk and PANTONE® products.

First Floor Eastgate House, 16–19 Eastcastle Street, London, W1W 8DA. Telephone: +44 (0) 20 7436 0133. Email: uksales@modeinfo.com.

Money Claim Online. Website: www.moneyclaim.gov.uk.

PANTONE® supplies the PANTONE® Colour System and other PANTONE products. Website: www.pantone.com.

Scottish Textile Industry Association is a gateway and guide to Scottish textile design and manufacturing and related information and assistance. Website: www.textilescotland.com.

UKFT UK Fashion & Textile Association is an independent trade association offering advice and help to designers, manufacturers and retailers in the UK. It runs the **Register of Apparel & Textile Designers** that gives help and advice for freelance designers at any stage of their development.
3 Queen Square, Bloomsbury, London, WC1N 3AR. Telephone: +44 (0) 20 7843 9460. For UKFT Email: info@ukft.org; for the Register of Apparel & Textile Designers Email: laurian.davies@ukft.org. Website: www.ukft.org.

UKFT Colour and Trend Library is by appointment only to UKFT member companies and current members of the UKFT Register of Apparel and Textile Designers.
Thomas Ramsden mill complex, Guiseley, LS20 9PD. Email: laurian.davies@ukft.org.

UK Courts. Website: www.hmcourts-service.gov.uk.

UK State Pension. Website: www.direct.gov.uk/en/Pensionsandretirementplanning.

UK Tax Credits. Helpline: 0845 300 3900. Website: www.direct.gov.uk/taxcredits.

UK Trade & Investment Enquiry Service is a government department that helps UK-based companies trade internationally and assists overseas companies to bring investment to the UK, providing knowledge, advice and practical support.
Europa Building, 450 Argyle Street, Glasgow, G2 8LH. Telephone: +44 (0) 20 7215 8000. Website: www.ukti.gov.uk.

Other organisations

The British Fashion Council promotes leading British fashion designers in a global market. It runs events that support and strengthen the UK's reputation for developing design excellence. These activities assist in the growth and economic impact of the designer fashion industry to UK PLC and enhance its international, cultural and creative reputation.
Somerset House, South Wing, Strand, London, WC2R 1LA. Website: www.britishfashion council.com.

Centre for Fashion Enterprise (CFE) is one of the world's leading strategic business development initiatives for emerging designer fashion labels, providing business incubation and high growth coaching.

182 Mare Street, London E8 3RE. Telephone: +44 (0) 20 7514 2295. Website: www.fashion-enterprise.com.

Morplan Ltd has stores in London, Enfield, Bristol and Glasgow that supply pattern-cutting and grading equipment and books. Telephone: 0800 45 11 22. Website: www.morplan.com.

Skillset Sector Skills Council (SSC) Skillset is the Creative Industries' Sector Skills Council. Its aim is to support the productivity of the Creative Industries to ensure that they remain globally competitive. Skillset does this by influencing and leading; developing skills, training and education policy; and through opening up the industries to the UK's pool of diverse talent.
Focus Point, 21 Caledonian Road, London, N1 9GB. Telephone: +44 (0) 20 7713 9800. Email: info@skillset.org. Website: www.skillset.org/fashion_and_textiles.

The Textile Institute is a registered charity comprising individual and corporate members in up to 80 countries. It aims to facilitate learning, recognise achievement, reward excellence and disseminate information.
1st floor, St James's Buildings, 79 Oxford Street, Manchester, M1 6FQ. Telephone: +44 (0) 161 237 1188. Email: tiihq@textileinst.org.uk. Website: www.textileinstitute.org.

Toolkits

The Creative Enterprise Toolkit contains tried and tested methods for creative individuals who are thinking about setting up a business. It provides guidance, activities, downloadable worksheets and case studies.
Website: www.nesta.org.uk/enterprise-toolkit- a guide for start-up fashion businesses in the UK: www.nesta.org.uk/library/documents/NESTA-CFE-Fashion-toolkit.pdf.

The Fashion Alliance Toolkit provides a series of toolkits created to help Fashion designers communicate their production needs clearly and effectively to manufacturing and production units.
Website: www.fashionalliance.co.uk/procurement_toolkit.php.

Index

accident and illness insurance 71
accommodation 53, 54, 94
accountancy 61–8
accountants 58–9
Adobe Illustrator 77, 118
advertising 35–6
advice, giving clients 55
agencies 5, 31, 34, 40
agents 11–12, 26
allowances 58, 62
alterations 12, 48, 49, 109
Anne Ritchie Consultancy 18, 38
Association of Suppliers to the British
    Clothing Industry (ASBCI) 38, 145, 165
AWI/Peclers 37

backing up work 100
bank accounts 50, 59–60
bankruptcy 85
Benhrima, Heather 6–7, 12, 19, 27, 29, 34,
    43, 45, 48, 110
Bishop, Paul 23
body rise measurement 152
body size charts 134–7
  flat measurements 150–1
  grade increments 119, 149, 151–2, 155,
    160–3
  maternity sizes 148
  'plus' sizes 147
  product development 110
  roughs 119
  tall and petite sizes 147
  'to fit' 11, 149, 153–4
  tolerance 153
  see also garment size charts
bookkeeping 61–8
branding 11, 76, 114

CADs 126–8
colour palette 113
confidentiality issues 78
design concept 110
full technical package 142
garment size charts 155
sample request forms 141
sizing differences 146
briefs 11, 109–10
British Fashion Council 166
buildings and contents insurance
    21, 71
Burns, Wendy 4, 58–9
Business Link 23, 61, 165
buyers 11, 19, 26

capital allowances 62
car insurance 71
catalogues 28, 145
Centre for Fashion Enterprise 166–7
cheques 82
children's sizing 144, 147, 151
Citizens' Advice Bureau 165
clients
  CAD templates 122–3
  contracts 74
  customer requirements 110–11, 113
  dealing with 30–2
  design briefs 109–10
  easy access to 18
  expectations 54–5
  face-to-face contact with 19, 31
  finding work 34–6, 38–9
  liaising with 11
  meeting with 21
  presentation of ideas to 115–16
  sizing issues 149, 152

clients (*Continued*)
  travelling abroad with 32, 53–4
  unreasonable demands from 92–4
climate 113
Clock In-Out Timesheet 95–6, 97
'cold calling' 35
college courses 102, 114
ColorMunki 112, 124
colour palette 113–14, 130
  CADs 123–4, 125, 126–8
  company profile 25
  design package calculator 49
  full technical package 141
colours
  CADs 125, 126–8, 130
  colour charts 110
  PANTONE colour system 23, 111–12, 124,
    125, 126–8, 130, 166
  restrictions on 111
  roughs 121
  sample request forms 137, 141
  UKFT Colour and Trend library 36–7,
    108, 166
Commercial Campaigns 22
company profile 25–6, 27, 38, 44
competition 5
  confidentiality issues 44
  ethics of working for competitors 78–9
  knowledge of competitors' ranges 28
complaints 54
computer-aided design (CAD) 10, 25
  presentation 11, 115, 118, 119, 121, 122,
    125–32, 142
  roughs 11, 119
  templates 122–3, 125, 128, 130
  training 37
  see also software
computer timesheets 94–9
computers 23
confidentiality issues 28, 44, 78–9
contacts 4, 9, 10, 34–5
contracts 14, 30, 51, 74–6
  cancelling 32
  design briefs 109

rates of pay 43
  small claims court 83
copyright issues 28, 30, 31, 44, 76–8
  branding 114
  CAD templates 122
  prosecution for breach of copyright 77–8
  'retention of title' clauses 51, 75, 76
  roughs 119
costs 39, 42, 44
  estimates and quotes 44, 48–51
  subcontracting 55
  travelling abroad 53
country differences 145–6
court action 83–5
covering letters 26–7, 38
Creative Enterprise Toolkit 167
Cridland, Marcus 29, 38, 40, 45
customer requirements 110–11, 113
Customs 93
'cut, make and trim' (CMT) 12
cutting patterns 6, 11–12, 20, 24, 26
CVs 25, 26, 27, 38, 44

date for annual accounts 61–2
Davies, Lauren 36, 92
deadlines 8, 9, 14, 15, 75, 94
degrees 9
delivery 12, 14, 51
Department for Business, Innovation
    & Skills 165
design briefs 11, 109–10
design development 11, 108–16, 118–42
  branding 114
  colour palette 113–14, 123–4
  company profile 25
  concept, style and shape 110–11
  design briefs 109–10
  detailed garment specifications 119,
    133–41, 142
  full technical package 141–2
  PANTONE colour system 111–12
  phases of a project 118–19
  presentation CADs 115, 118, 119, 121,
    122, 125–32, 142

presentation of ideas to client 115–16
research and trends 108–9
roughs 115, 119–22
tickets and labels 114–15
design package calculator 49
design rights 76–7
detailing
CADs 119, 123, 126–30
design package calculator 49
detailed garment specifications 11, 119,
133–41, 142
sample request forms 141
diaries 40, 89
dressing 28–30, 43

email 19, 31, 48
distractions 91
roughs 122
sending work by 51
embroidery
CADs 128, 129
roles and responsibilities 11
sample request forms 138, 139,
141, 142
specialists 10
EMTEX Limited Designer Forum 37, 108,
118, 165
equipment 23, 24
estimates 44, 48–51
ethical issues 78–9
ethnicity 113
EU law 77, 79
Excel grade charts 134–7, 142, 145, 148,
149, 153–63
see also garment size charts
expenditure charts 64–8
expenses 39, 41, 42, 44
accounting 58
advance funds 93
contract terms 75
deductable 62
estimates 48, 49, 50
invoicing 52
receipts 61

record keeping 89
travelling abroad 53
experience 10

fabrics
buying 12
colour palette 113
garment size charts 155
sample request forms 137, 138,
139, 141
selecting 11
face-to-face contact 19, 31
family life 21, 23, 91
Faresin, Nina 4
Fashion Alliance Toolkit 167
fastenings 137, 138, 139, 141
fees 39, 40–3
contract terms 75
estimates and quotes 44, 48–51
hourly rates 9, 40, 50, 75
season rates 50
travelling abroad 53–4
UK/Netherlands comparison 5
see also payment
files 48–9, 51, 77
finance 8, 9, 58–71
bank accounts 59–60
bookkeeping and accountancy 61–8
choosing an accountant 58–9
employing staff 70–1
income tax 60–1
insurance 71
National Insurance contributions 69, 70
pension provision 70
see also fees; payment
finding work 34–6, 38–9
fixed fee quotes 49
flexibility 4, 6, 7
freelance working 4–15
advantages of 7
decision to become freelance 4, 8–9
disadvantages of 7–8
experience 10
qualifications 9–10

freelance working (*Continued*)
  skills and abilities 10–13
  working in London 5–6
full technical package 141–2

garment size charts 134–7, 149–52,
    155–63
  see also body size charts; Excel grade
    charts
garment specifications 119, 133–41, 142
  company profile 26
  design package calculator 49
  roles and responsibilities 11
garment technologists 11–12
grade charts 119, 134–7, 142, 145, 148,
    149, 153–63
grade increments 119, 149, 151–2, 155,
    160–3
graders 11–12
grading 11, 24
graphic designers 11–12
graphics 10, 26, 114

hand-drawn roughs 119–20
Harrison, Shirley 19, 21, 24, 28, 29, 40, 44,
    49, 58
health and safety 71
Health and Safety Executive (HSE) 71, 165
Heimtextil 37
higher neck point (HNP) 133, 151
HM Revenue & Customs (HMRC) 58, 60, 61,
    69, 70, 71, 165
holidays 89–90
home, working from 7, 20–1, 23, 88, 90–1
Hours Log Timesheet 96–9

illustrations 11, 115
income charts 62–4, 65
income tax 60–1
indemnity insurance 59, 71
Inspired Business Solutions 34
insurance 21, 59, 71
intellectual property rights 49, 76–7
  see also copyright issues

Internet
  Internet service providers 24
  liaising with buyers and factories 19
  research and trends 108
  sizing information 145
  working from home 21
  see also websites
interviews 28, 29–30, 39, 43–5
invoicing 51–3
  chasing outstanding invoices 82
  record keeping 61
  season rates 50

jury service 90

Kasbah 6

lab dips 12
labels 79, 114–15, 130, 137, 138, 139, 141
ladieswear 13
Learning and Skills Improvement Service
    (LSIS) 103, 165
legal issues
  confidentiality 78–9
  contracts 74–6
  experts 79
  late payment 82–3
  public liability insurance 21, 71
  renting a studio 22
  UK and EU law 77, 79
  see also copyright issues
life insurance 71
limited companies 58–9
loans 59–60
location, selecting a 18–20
logos 78, 114, 123, 138, 139
London 5–6, 18, 19, 20
loneliness 8, 13
loose-fitting garments 111

machinists 11–12
magazine images 30, 77–8, 116
magazines, as source of trend
    information 108

manufacturers 11–12, 26
Masters of Linen 37
maternity sizes 148
measurements 134–7
  flat 150–1
  garment size charts 155, 159
  grade increments 151–2
  'to fit' 11, 144, 145, 148, 149,
    153–4, 155
  tolerance 153
  see also sizing
Mode Information 108, 165–6
Money Claim Online 83, 84, 166
MoOD 37
mood boards 28, 30, 77–8, 108, 115, 116
Morplan Ltd 167
motivation 9, 13, 30
Mudpie 37

National Insurance contributions (NICs)
    69, 70
Nelly Rodi 37
Netherlands 5–6, 18
networking 4, 34, 35, 36

O'Callaghan, Tim 74, 76
organisational skills 6
out-of-court settlements 84

PANTONE colour system 23, 111–12, 124,
    125, 126–8, 130, 166
part-time teaching 13, 102–4
patents 79
patterns
  CADs 128–30
  cutting 6, 11–12, 20, 24, 26
payment
  into bank accounts 50
  chasing outstanding invoices 82
  contract terms 75
  invoicing 51–3
  late or non-payment 8, 74, 75, 82–5
  receiving 52–3
  see also fees; finance

pension provision 70
petite sizes 147
photographs 28, 77–8
plans 41–2
'plus' sizes 144, 147
politeness 54
portfolios 27–8, 44
pregnant women 148
Premiere Vision 37
presentation CADs 11, 115, 118, 119, 121,
    122, 125–32, 142
press releases 36
Presstige 23
Prince's Trust 59
print design
  company profile 26
  roles and responsibilities 11
  specialists 10
print details 128, 129, 141
product development teams 11
production, overseeing 12
professional organisations 36–8
  advice and guidance from 13, 40, 79
  finding work 34
  training courses 102
project phases 118–19
public liability insurance 21, 71

qualifications 9–10, 103
quality control 12, 14–15
quotes 44, 48–51

rates of pay see fees
receipts 61
recommendations and referrals 38
Register of Apparel and Textile Designers
    34, 36, 37
renting a studio 21–3
reputation 14
research 11, 19–20, 108–9
  client's products 110
  company profile 25
  contacting companies 34–5, 43
  design package calculator 49

research (*Continued*)
  mood boards 28
  project phases 118
  sizing information 145
'retention of title' clauses 51, 75, 76
retirement 70
rib detail 130, 132, 138, 139, 142
Ritchie, Anne 18–19
Robertson, David 90, 147, 150
roles and responsibilities 10, 11–12
roughs 11, 115, 119–22, 141
royalties 92

sales teams 11
sales techniques 38–9
sample request forms 119, 137–41, 142
samples
  equipment 24
  making 11, 20
  sealing 12
  sizing issues 152
Scottish Textile Industry Association 38,
    108, 166
season rates 50
Self-Assessment Returns 60, 62
self-discipline 9, 13, 30, 88, 90
seminars
  sizing information 145
  training 102
  trend 108
serviced premises 22–3
shape 110–11, 144
Shires Equestrian Products 29
Shirley Harrison Fashion Design 19
sizing 11, 144–64
  access to current information 145–6
  country differences 145–6
  design package calculator 49
  differences between companies 146–7
  Excel grade charts 134–7, 145, 148, 149,
    153–63
  flat measurements 150–1
  garment size charts 134–7, 150–2,
    155–63

grade increments 119, 149, 151–2, 155,
    160–3
  issues with 144–5
  maternity sizes 148
  'plus' sizes 144, 147
  pre-production sampling 152
  product development 110
  roughs 119
  sample request forms 137, 141
  tall and petite sizes 147
  'to fit' body measurements 11, 144, 145,
    148, 149, 153–4, 155
  tolerance 153
  see also body size charts
skills 6, 9, 10–13, 25, 26, 28
Skillset Sector Skills Council (SSC) 167
skin tone 113
small claims court 83–5
Small Earnings Exception (SEE) 69
Smartway Consulting Ltd 13
Smink, Marianne 5–6, 18
social networking sites 35
software 23
  Adobe Illustrator 77, 118
  ColorMunki 112, 124
  training courses 102, 118
  see also computer-aided design; Excel
    grade charts
solicitors 74, 85
Spain 18–19
specialisation 5, 10, 55
spreadsheets
  bookkeeping 62–8
  timesheets 95–9
  see also Excel grade charts
staff, employing 70–1
stationery 25
storage space 21, 24
storyboards 115–16
stripes 128–31, 142
studios 21–3
style numbers 119, 125, 141, 155
Stylesight 37
subcontracting 10, 55

sueing 59
suppliers 11–12, 38
swatches 111
swing tickets 114–15, 130, 132, 142

tall sizes 147
Tatnell, Suzie 22
tax issues
  accounting 58
  business expenses calculator 42
  income tax 60–1
  loans 59
teaching 13, 103–4
tear-off paper chips (TPX) 111
technical specifications 11, 26, 28
  see also garment specifications
telephone calls 19, 23, 24, 31
  charging for 89
  'cold calling' 35
  costs 39
  distractions 91
  telephone manner 38
  working from home 21
templates
  CAD presentation 122–3, 125, 128, 130
  Excel garment size charts 146, 149–50,
    155–9
  expenditure charts 64–8
  garment 125
  income charts 62–4, 65
  invoices 52
  roughs 120–1
  sample request forms 140–1
  'to fit' body measurement charts 153–4
Textile Institute 167
Textile Market Intelligence Trend presentations 38
tickets 114–15, 130, 132, 142
tight-fitting garments 111
time management 8, 88–100
  backing up work 100
  calculating the length of a project 48–9
  computer timesheets 94–9
  diaries 89

holidays 89–90
interruptions and distractions 90–1
part-time teaching 103–4
unreasonable demands 92–4
working day 88–9
timesheets 94–9
tiredness 93
'to fit' body measurements 11, 144, 145,
  148, 149, 153–4, 155
toiles 11
tolerance 153, 155
trade references 82
trade shows 19, 20, 104
  finding work 35, 39
  research and trends 109
  travelling with others to 13
  trend books 37
trademarks 76, 78, 79
training 9, 10, 37, 102, 114, 118
travel 18, 19, 20, 89
  car insurance 71
  part-time teaching and 103, 104
  travelling abroad 32, 53–4, 93–4
  travelling with others 13
trend boards 30, 77, 108, 115, 116
trends 11, 108–9
  EMTEX Limited Designer Forum 37
  Textile Market Intelligence Trend
    presentations 38
  UKFT Colour and Trend library 36–7
trimmings
  buying 12
  CADs 124, 126
  design 11
  equipment 24
  garment size charts 155
  sample request forms 137, 141
  selecting 11
trust 6

UK Fashion and Textile Association (UKFT)
  34, 36–7, 77, 79, 166
UK Trade and Investment Enquiry Service
  166

UKFT Colour and Trend library 36–7,
        108, 166
university courses 102

value added tax (VAT) 52, 60, 69, 75
'vanity sizing' 146

Walker, Chris 34, 108, 109, 115–16
Walker, Michelle 148
wardrobe, choosing a 28–30
washing requirements 113, 137, 141
websites 24, 27, 28
    finding work 35–6
    useful 165–7
    see also Internet

Wendy Burns Designs Ltd 4
Wilson, Emma 13, 14, 133, 137
work-life balance 88–9
working hours 7, 41, 89
    computer timesheets 94–9
    travelling abroad 53
    unreasonable 54, 93–4
working space 21

year plans 41–2